GROWING INTO FAITH

GROWING INTO FAITH

GERARD RUMMERY, FSC
DAMIAN LUNDY, FSC

Darton, Longman and Todd
London

First published in 1982
Darton, Longman and Todd Ltd
89 Lillie Road
London SW6 1UD

© 1982 Gerard Rummery
Damian Lundy

ISBN 0 232 51482 8

British Library Cataloguing in Publication Data

Rummery, Gerard
  Growing into faith.
  1. Religious education
  I. Title   II. Lundy, Damian
  207   BV1471.2

ISBN 0–232–51482–8

Phototypeset by
Input Typesetting Ltd, London SW19 8DR
Printed in Great Britain by
The Anchor Press Ltd
and bound by Wm Brendon & Son Ltd
both of Tiptree, Essex

CONTENTS

PREFACE

In this book we have tried to include many insights from our reading and research, and from our personal experience of working with young people and adults in several countries. In inviting you to read and share these insights, we would like to encourage you to use the book as a way of reflecting on your own experience – the journey of faith that you have made and are still making with others. You will be invited to explore many questions, some of which are very personal, all of which seem to us to be important for today's Catholics – and especially for all who exercise pastoral responsibility as parents, teachers, catechists or leaders of communities.

You may explore these issues alone, but we hope you will discover that it is usually more fruitful to share the task with others, for instance in small groups. If a number of you meet together for this purpose, in helping one another to become more aware of the questions we raise, you will appreciate the contention which lies behind this book: that there are no simple, universally applicable answers to the important questions we are considering. As the twentieth century moves towards the twenty-first, old and young alike are pilgrims together, and in our changing society and Church it is no longer a case of confused young searchers asking their questions to which older, wiser believers trot out the obvious familiar answers to be found, in a more stable age, in the common catechism, or in the standard manuals of theology, or in the positions adopted within the traditional bastions of a centralized, unchanging, uniform Church.

In adopting this attitude, we believe that we are being faithful not only to our times but to the very nature of faith itself, and to the experience of the first Christian believers. We believe that people are called to make the journey of faith not by treading mechanically a predetermined path, but rather by responding personally to the call of Christ who invited disciples to follow him

vii

and who sent these followers into different parts of the known world to establish communities of believers. He did not equip them with a neat collection of prepackaged revealed truths. They had experienced for themselves the good news of what God has done for everyone in Jesus, and they were empowered by his Spirit to carry this message so that others could make it their own. This is how local churches were established.

In our more complex changing society, the domestic church of the family still nurtures faith. Catholic institutions like schools and parishes still play their part, however inadequately. But *all* believers, whatever their age or situation, need other communities, some perhaps of a transient nature, which point the direction and offer strength and support to pilgrims at different stages of their journey. It is our hope that the community you will become in working through this book together, in reflecting, searching, praying and celebrating, will help each of you grow into a stronger, more mature faith.

We have worked on this book during the year which commemorated the foundation, three hundred years ago, by St John Baptist de la Salle and his followers, of a little school in Rheims – the first of many places of learning opened by the Brothers of the Christian Schools to help young people grow into faith.

Finally a word of thanks to Gabriel Barnfield, FSC for his help with the diagrams included in the text and to Vincent Kilty, FSC for the cover photograph of young people at St Cassian's Centre, Kintbury.

Gerard Rummery FSC
Damian Lundy FSC

Ascension Day,
May 28, 1981

ACKNOWLEDGEMENTS

Thanks are due to Darton, Longman and Todd Ltd and Double-day and Co. Inc. for permission to reproduce material from *The Jerusalem Bible* © 1966, 1967 and 1968.

Also to Macmillan, London and Basingstoke, for permission to reproduce the following material by R. S. Thomas, 'The Kingdom' from *H'm* (1972) and 'The Moon in Lleyn' from *Laboratories of the Spirit* (1975).

1

GROWING INTO FAITH IN A
CHANGING WORLD

To grow *into* faith?

This may sound strange to people who think of themselves, baptized in infancy, as having received the gift of faith from God, given through the Church's sacrament, so that it might grow in them during the years of childhood. The seed will grow into a tender plant, bearing spring blossoms and first fruits, if it is cultivated and protected in the faith-filled atmosphere of a caring home and a good Catholic school. Then comes the crisis – the stormy season of adolescence with its dangerous and destructive questioning, doubting and disillusionment, when the young plant is ravaged by the blight of apathy and by the withering blasts of cynicism and irreligion which blow across the wasteland of a materialistic and godless age.

We could explore this caricature with the aid of other images. Some think of faith as a precious gift, to be treasured, protected by devotional practices, as the recipient crosses the deserts of adolescence into the new and challenging world of adult life; in this desert lurk many robbers and bandits, watching to attack the poor traveller, who, having robbed him of his gift, leave him for dead or compel him to join them in the raiding-parties and ambushes destined for future victims. A few travellers escape unharmed, but in this violent age when muggings have become commonplace, most young Catholics seem to fall among thieves. There are some Good Samaritans, but not enough. And Mother Church stands helplessly, looking on, like Rachel weeping for her children because they are not.

To grow *into* faith – not to 'keep' or protect the faith already received, but to grow gradually into faith – is for many Catholics an unfamiliar and challenging way of thinking. To grow into faith

1

implies becoming more open to God, more receptive to his word, more responsive to his call, more faithful to his service. We are asked not so much to defend or protect the faith we have already received (as if it is a 'thing', say a body of beliefs, inside us), but to develop attitudes of openness, honest searching, sensitivity to God's word, and concern for others – to become a good traveller, ready to trust and to endure, prepared to make the journey of a lifetime.

Today, many theologians speak of faith as 'a person's response to God's revelation', rather than as a collection of revealed truths to be accepted unquestioningly and defended vigorously. This is not a complete definition, but it is a helpful starter. To speak of God's revelation is to think of God's activity in our regard as being summarized in three key verbs which we find in Scripture and which help us to unlock much of what the Bible contains:

> God speaks;
> God calls;
> God saves.

The verbs are in the present tense. After listening to the readings during a Eucharist we are invited to respond thankfully to the sentence: 'This is the word of the Lord.' NOT 'That *was* the word of the Lord' two thousand years ago. Christians are those who hear the word of God and keep it, and a central Christian belief is that God still speaks, as he spoke to our fathers through the prophets, as he spoke in Jesus, his Word made flesh. If our God speaks, then certain questions arise:

> When does he speak?
> How does he speak?
> What does he say?
> To whom does he speak today?

For many people, present and former believers, God's favourite word is 'No', but St Paul (2 Corinthians 1: 17–22) says the opposite: he describes Jesus as 'God's YES', the YES to all God's promises made to us. If we don't hear God speaking this word to us, it may be because we don't know how to listen to him. We might need to think of prayer as listening to God, instead of as speaking to him. This is a skill to be acquired. I need someone to show me. I need an older, more experienced fellow-pilgrim, one who can offer me some spiritual direction for my journey.

Who calls me to make the journey? The God who speaks, for he is also a God who *calls*.

2

His word is a call: 'Hear, O Israel. . . .' God calls me by name. A call is a word addressed to a person or to a group. It may be an invitation or a challenge. It demands a response. 'Faith' is the word used to describe a person's response to God's call, and to describe the attitude which makes such a response possible. The call is addressed to the whole person, not just to the mind, but more especially to the heart. A person's response is shown by attitudes and actions, not by lip-service or intellectual assent. The Bible speaks of man's response to God's word, our acceptance of God's acceptance of us, as a 'covenant'. In Jesus, God calls to the whole human race, offering a new and everlasting covenant, a new and healing relationship for everyone who wants to accept it.

God speaks to us and calls to us in order to *save* us. Left to ourselves, we turn our lives and our relationships into junk-yards. We are victims of history and of our own sins. We cannot save ourselves, but by listening and responding to God's healing word we are saved from our fear, our distress, our crippling sense of worthlessness, our deafness, blindness, and paralysis. The saving word of God is therefore good news. In the Old Testament, God's saving action is explored in many images – in the actions of a shepherd, a mother, a father, a deliverer, which offer metaphors of God's concern for his people, a concern which is illustrated most vividly in the Jewish experience of Exodus and in the journey to the promised land: a time of testing and growth:

> You grumbled in your tents. 'It is because he hates us,' you said, 'that Yahweh brought us out of the land of Egypt to put us under the power of the Amorites and so destroy us. What kind of a place are we making for? Our own brothers have made us lose heart: It is a people, they say, bigger and stronger than we are; their cities are immense, with walls reaching to the sky. . . And I (Moses) said to you: 'Do not take fright, do not be afraid of them. Yahweh your God goes in front of you and will be fighting on your side as you saw him fight for you in Egypt. In the wilderness too, you saw him: how Yahweh carried you, as a man carries his child, all along the road you travelled on the way to this place. But for all this, you put not faith in Yahweh your God, who had gone in front of you on the journey to find you a camping ground, by night in the fire to light your path, by day in the cloud.
>
> (Deuteronomy 1: 27ff)

Gradually, people came to understand that God's healing and liberating action (which we call 'salvation') is for everyone – God has no favourites (Acts 10: 34ff). This is revealed in the life of Jesus, whose name means 'Saviour', and whose healing actions fill the pages of the Gospels. These signs are new metaphors of concern, to be translated into the present tense so that we can see and experience them as images of what he can do for us today in our blindness, dumbness, deafness, and half-dead state. God's word is powerful in that it enlightens, empowers, heals, awakens, liberates, and reassures. How does God save us? By speaking to us and by calling us. How are we saved? By listening and responding to his word. This may take a long time to realize. In the Bible, ideas about God evolve until they can all be summed up in the single verb: God *loves* (1 John 4:16).

But where is Jesus now? Where is the saving love to be found? The answer is surprising and not immediately obvious: God's Word made flesh, incarnate now, is to be found in the communities to whom the good news has been entrusted, in whom the Spirit of Jesus lives and works. These communities of Jesus' followers are called 'Church', although we might find it hard to identify the institutions familiar to us as these communities of the good news and the Spirit. To grow into faith is a challenge to grow into Church. I do not believe alone; I do not make the journey of faith alone. 'WE believe.' I am baptized into the faith of the community, and as I grow I look to my fellow-Christians to be accepted, nourished, forgiven, healed, blessed, renewed, challenged and enlightened, so that I in my turn, with my brothers and sisters, may become the good news which will save the world.

The problem of being Church is the problem of trying to become what we claim to be, what we are called to be. In our age, for many people (non-believers or ex-believers) the Church appears to reject, condemn, act blindly, building up fear, enslaving, hiding God, restricting him instead of revealing him. And yet we claim to be the good news of what God is like! Where do many people get their false and frightening images of God? From a Church which fails in its mission to manifest the accepting, loving, forgiving, liberating 'good news' God, whom Jesus told us to call 'Abba'. Regrettably, this negative view of Church is often the experience of adolescents today. A commission researching the attitudes of young people in England towards Church and faith found that the factor most influencing rejection and disaffection was the Church itself, the institution which is condemned as 'dead boring', as having nothing to offer to the young. An essential task for all those concerned to answer the question: 'Will our children have

4

faith?' is to become involved with the renewal of the faith-community we call 'Church' and to face such questions as:

Why is Church a problem today?
Why especially is Church usually unattractive to adolescents?
Why is the whole situation a problem for parents, teachers, and
    pastors?
How can these areas of crisis become growth-points for young
    people, for their teachers and parents, and for the entire
    church community?

There are no easy solutions, but at least we can explore the problems and look for new opportunities, and become part of the whole process of reform and renewal which is the continuing work of the Second Vatican Council. Pope John XXIII prayed that the Council would be a new Pentecost for all Christians. But not all Christians responded enthusiastically to the prospect of far-reaching changes. Many still resist, and feel threatened. Why? Let us explore this question in some detail. To do so, we must explore not only our Church, but also our society, for we belong to the twentieth century – a society marked by radical change.

To live is to change

Our lives have been a continuing process of discovery, of enlargement of our possibilities for growth, physical mobility, speech and other forms of communication. The gradual assumption of our own autonomy[1] (however 'controlled' this may have been initially) was probably most rapid at a time of our lives when physical changes in our bodies reminded us of our adult status and of our potential for parenthood. The choices of that period which took us to a particular kind of work, the choice of a stable way of life with a marriage partner, the assumption of responsibility for another person and later for the generation and care of children, all involved us in the continuing process of change. Resistance to change or a general suspicion of it is often something which appears in us in middle age when the main directions of our lives have been well-established, but I would like to try to analyse some particular aspects of change which seem more marked in our

[1] This word is being used throughout this book with the meaning of 'the general move towards personal independence and responsibility which is most consistent with the dignity of human beings'.

western societies now than at any previous period of history. These are fundamental changes which affect the lives of all of us and cause particular difficulties between people of different generations.

Three kinds of societies[2]

Our lives are bound by time and space. In a nomadic kind of society, we could represent the relationship between time and space by means of a straight line like this:

Yesterday   Today   Tomorrow   Oasis   Next week   Future time

Perhaps there is a yearly or more seasonal cycle to this pattern, but in general the nomad does not plant crops, so that his pattern of return is determined by his more immediate needs and his knowledge of where he can find food and water.

A society which lives on agriculture is better represented by a circle.

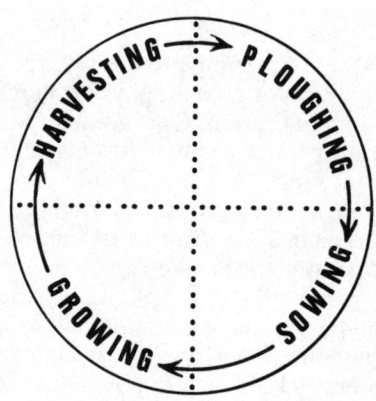

[2] In the analysis which follows the diagrams are based on those used by Pierre Moitel in *Demain est déjà aujourd'hui* (Centurion, Paris, 1978).

Within the compass of the year there are the seasons for planting and sowing, for tending and caring, for reaping and harvesting. This means as well the putting down of physical roots. Homes are to be built and barns are to be constructed because this particular use of time makes new demands on the use of space as well. The encompassing circle of time becomes soon the circle of the home with its walls, the grouping of homes in the village, the walled town and city which offers security and protection. For many centuries, this pattern of living tended to limit the outside contacts of the circle-dwellers to the demands of times and seasons. There were also 'nomadic' merchants who made journeys, but even these depended on the regular needs of the circle-dwellers.

Modern city living has many of the qualities of the circle but the phenomenon of increased mobility gives it a breadth and flexibility which transcend many traditional aspects of time and space. Electric light can turn night into day. Time can be organized into 'work shifts' which ensure that expensive machinery is never idle. Space can be conquered by the personal mobility provided by the car and by the jet plane. Human beings have many centres of living. We may call this way of living 'many-centred' (or poly-nuclear) and represent it thus:

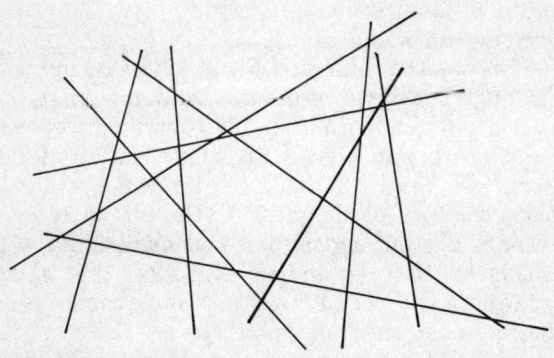

In modern society there are many centres among which we share various parts of ourselves and our lives. We live in one place but we can work (because of transport) in another; we can enjoy our sport or our music or our plays in another; our children can have schools, or friends or activities which are 'centres' which touch little of our lives; we can take 'foreign' holidays perhaps for little more than we would have spent once in staying at the seaside. We are aware, through radio and television, of happenings in other parts of the world almost as soon as the people themselves there; we can remain in touch, through post and telephone, with friends who live on the other side of the world. In this complex modern society, we have a wide range of choices open to us which previous generations never enjoyed.

Our modern society still has nomads. Some are so because the changes which have influenced the development of other societies have not affected them. There are also modern 'nomads' who have resisted the pressure of a modern city-based way of living to seek a simpler form of society. Some of these we have called 'hippies' or 'drop-outs' because they have deliberately sought to be no longer members of a modern western-style society. Some of us still know the kind of life devoted to farming and agriculture, and it is interesting (and perhaps significant?) that we sometimes choose to spend vacations working, or living simply, as perhaps our grandparents did. But in the West generally, the choices open to us are largely those offered by the many-centred society. And the key word here is very important: it is the choices which often make all the difference.

In reflecting on social change and its implications, the well-known anthropologist, Margaret Mead, offers us an important set of distinctions.[3] She distinguishes three different kinds of cultures: one in which children learn primarily from their forebears ('postfigurative'), a second in which both children and adults learn from their peers ('cofigurative'), and a third in which adults learn also from their children ('prefigurative'). The first of these describes both the nomadic and agricultural communities for it is 'one in which change is so slow and imperceptible that grandparents, holding newborn grandchildren in their arms, cannot conceive any other future for the children than their own lives'.[4]

This probably has not been the situation for many of us with regard to our grandparents. It is certainly not the case for children

[3] *Culture and Commitment*, a study of the Generation Gap Based on the Man and Nature lectures, March 1969 (Panther Books, St Albans, 1972), p. 31.
[4] Ibid.

born in western society today. For some of us, our experience would seem to be better described by Margaret Mead's second idea (a 'cofigurative culture') a situation 'in which the experience of the young generation is radically different from that of their parents, grandparents and the older members of their immediate community . . . (for) their progenitors can provide them with no living models suitable for their age. They themselves must develop new styles based on their own experience and provide models for their own peers.'[5] If we consider our different level of education, career, place of living, experience of travel, means of communication, sources of information and in general, our possibilities for choice, we may feel that so much of this has indeed been 'radically different' from that of our parents and, even more so, of our grandparents.

But the rapidity of social change has not simply left us on some new stable plateau of achievement. Already, the second culture co-exists with Margaret Mead's third category (a prefigurative culture) because '. . . in this new culture it will be the child – and not the parent or grandparent – that represents what is to come. Instead of the erect, white-haired elder who . . . stood for the past and the future in all their grandeur and continuity, the unborn child, already conceived but still in the womb, must become a symbol of what life will be like.'[6] In our modern culture with its complex use of space and time, we cannot really predict a future for the children yet to be born. Creative artists, projecting from their perception of some tendencies in society, have frightened us with the horrifying possibilities of an Orwellian *1984*, of Huxley's *Brave New World*, and of a whole host of plays and TV series which envisage Doomsday. We can feel ourselves powerless against all kinds of changes which threaten us precisely because they seem capricious and unpredictable. As adults, as parents, we sometimes wonder whether we have anything to say to a younger generation which faces a future of which we have had no experience.

The generally conserving forces of our society – government, schools, the Church – seem to have faltered in the face of this rapidity of change, leaving us without the certainties which such institutions once offered. Increased knowledge of other lands and of other customs (facilitated by our radios and television screens) can seem to make relative many values which we once thought of as fundamental. We experience pluralism. Our insistence on cer-

[5] Ibid., p. 64.
[6] Ibid., p. 110.

tain standards of conduct which we have always held as 'right' is challenged by younger people who are aware that others do not observe them. The pluralism of values in a modern society denies us the support of custom and tradition and seems to make such values relative or simply the object of free choice. In practice, there are many possible models for young people, not simply one.

Even the Church has changed. . . .

For many of us there is the fairly fresh memory of a Church which stood 'rock in strength upon the rock . . . braving storm and earthquake shock', as the once-familiar hymn expressed it. Sweeping changes have led to the almost complete disappearance of a Latin liturgy which served the western Church for so many centuries. There have been so many changes in what was once 'fixed' and 'certain': schools once run exclusively by religious sisters, brothers, or priests have now passed over to lay teachers; many traditional hymns and forms of devotion have gone out of favour; often priests and religious are no longer at all times immediately identifiable by their distinctive dress; fidelity to marriage vows and to priestly or religious celibacy seems less honoured than it was in the past; the recent National Pastoral Congress in England seems to have questioned so many practices which once defined Catholics against modern society. Each of us could continue the list.

Four ways of being 'Catholic'[7]

All of this is certainly true, at least if one simply looks at the factual aspects of change. For many decades, the enduring 'model' Catholic was the kind of person we described simply as 'a good Catholic'. The term was an all-embracing one. It described the person who attended Mass on Sundays and feasts as the Church required, who observed the laws of the Church as regards Christian marriage, that is, the procreation of children and the education of such children through the Catholic schools. The 'good Catholic' was active but submissive in church activities and loyal to support

[7] The following analysis follows and adapts that of Jacques Audinet in an article, 'Catechesis: the Church building the Church in a given culture', in *Our Apostolate*, vol. 24, no. 3 (August 1976).

its works by financial aid and defence of its policies and doctrines. The example of such people was often reckoned one of the most powerful factors attracting converts to Catholicism. In the Catholic Church one could find certainty.

There were, of course, other ways of being Catholic. A second group, the people whom we would call 'militant', frequently worked in the labour movement to ensure that Catholic social teaching was known and applied. Often these 'militants' devoted their lives to combating the spread of Communism in trade unions and similar organizations. Other militants spoke out for the Church through the Catholic Evidence Guilds and similar activities, while others quietly (and often anonymously) served the needs of Christ's poor through groups such as the St Vincent de Paul society and the Legion of Mary.

A third group had that 'mystical' approach to Catholicism which stressed the importance of devotion, contemplation and quiet prayer. This was often tied to the quiet of the early morning Mass ('the blessed mutter of the Mass'), to visits to the Blessed Sacrament at different opportunities through the day, and to the personal devotion of the rosary. In more recent years, many Catholics have found their lives deepened through their coming into contact with the charismatic prayer groups, with their stress on the reading of the Bible and on forms of shared prayer and the singing of hymns. Of course, these categories were not necessarily so separate. 'Good' Catholics could be both 'militant' and 'mystical', but the general types described were recognizable in Catholic communities.

In more recent years we seem to have become aware of the coming of somebody whom we might call the 'secularized Christian'. The move from 'Catholic' to 'Christian' is significant. One of the forerunners of this movement was the Lutheran pastor and writer, Dietrich Bonhoeffer, who while imprisoned in Nazi Germany wrote prophetically of the coming age of what he called 'religionless Christianity'. This new 'secularized Christian' may be deeply concerned with the issues of today but he does not find much support for them in the Catholic Church he has known. He is interested to share and work with fellow-Christians when he finds them more concerned with such issues than he finds his fellow-Catholics. Perhaps his education makes him question many aspects of church teaching as he hears it expounded. His own experience of life makes him impatient with a hierarchically structured Church which offers him no more personal autonomy as an adult than it did for him as a child. He is often interested and partly informed on modern expressions of Catholic teaching (e.g. the Vatican II documents and commentaries on them), but finds little resonance from this in parish life. He may well drop out of regular connection with the Church or choose to attend services where he finds something which is more satisfying or closer to the reality of life as he experiences it. He 'shops around' for a Mass where he feels more at home with himself and his family. If he does not find it, he loses contact with the Church of his upbringing.

Some connections. . .

There are some important connections to be made between these four 'types' and the different kinds of society sketched earlier. The enduring image of 'the good Catholic' was particularly associated with the stable rural or neighbourhood parish where there was an easily identifiable Catholic sub-culture. Often grouped together because of various forms of discrimination practised against them, Catholics found and maintained their identity by uniting against opposition. The passionate loyalties that were developed in 'proving' that Catholics were so serious about their claims for separate schools that they would build and finance their own, gave people a pride and a stake in the success of such a school and its pupils. It was so, too, with the cathedrals and the parish churches built with 'the pennies of the poor'. In this Catholic sub-culture (as with comparable ethnic groups today), Catholics were expected to marry Catholics, they consulted Catholic doctors, they preferred (where they existed) Catholic hospitals and nurses, they supported Catholic schools. There were Catholic societies for young people and business organizations and insurance firms which attracted Catholic support. The achievements of Catholics were rejoiced in by fellow-Catholics, often with a certain exaggeration which may have justified the satirical quotation from a radical Catholic paper which read: 'Catholic cow wins butterfat award!'

This kind of society had room for the 'good Catholic', the 'militant Catholic' and the 'mystical Catholic'. It is a sign of its vitality that such types were recognizable, and are probably still so where that kind of culture and society exist. It is the society of the circle and it is most clearly Margaret Mead's 'postfigurative' culture. When the experience of the young becomes radically different (through the social, physical and financial mobility

12

achieved through their sub-culture), then the 'cofigurative' society is also present. We recognize the person of this age in the very root sense of the word 'secular'; the 'secularized Christian' has arrived but co-exists with the 'good', the 'militant' and the 'mystical', at least in a contemporary sense, precisely because of the mobility which is possible in a modern society with many centres. What concerns us as parents and teachers, however, is to know how our generation can help our children, born into a pre-figurative culture, but facing a different future. To do this, I suggest, we must first deepen our analysis as to *what* has changed and *why*.

From being the same to being different. . .

A stable culture provided us with an identity. Armed with the tools of the alphabet and grammar and dictionaries, with the logic and precision of mathematical tables, we have been particularly successful in *repeating* and *reproducing* (consider, for example the historical impact of the printing press in European culture!), and so the culture and society we have known have been marked by order and a certain hierarchy of importance. In many ways, however, what have become the stereotypes of the 'pre-determined' and the 'pre-established' have been challenged today by more emphasis on the importance of the individual, and the acceptance and celebration of differences. By its very nature, such an attitude can be dismissed as leading to anarchy or to a cult of 'personalism', but it need not be necessarily so negative. It may be, in terms of our earlier analysis, a continuing search for meaning in a universe where today's adults can no longer predict the future in terms of their particular past.

One example will suffice. In an article entitled, 'In what kind of universe are we?', a French priest and writer quotes the following observation of a modern expert on communications:

At the rate learning is expanding, the amount of knowledge will be four times more important than it ever was when a child, born today, leaves University. When the child will be fifty years old, 97% of what he has learned will have been invented since the day he was born.[8]

The continuing problem is one of relevance. There can be no longer simply the weight of tradition to justify traditional learning.

[8] Pierre Moitel, *Word in Life*, vol. 27, no. 3, p. 69.

The very explosion of knowledge highlights our necessity of providing young people with the skills to obtain access to the sources of knowledge rather than expecting them to know everything themselves. It is not only that the child no longer knows the old values. More seriously, he may not have experienced the process of apprenticeship to the new. The new culture based on 'difference' will necessarily place more stress on the idea of relationships. At its very best it will highlight the importance of the individual, of creativity, of continuing evolution; at its worst, it may so relativize everything that nothing assumes any importance, and the individual is lost on a vast landscape where there are no longer any landmarks. This kind of Kafka-esque scenario has already been explored in many ways by creative writers and artists. Does the Church, so easily identified with the concentric patterns of the circle and the cultures associated with it, have a role in this world where the many-centred culture is already continuing its increasing rate of change? Put another way, can the Church transcend the cultural forms it has assumed in its history so as to be more obviously relevant to this new society?

For reflection and group discussion

1. Modern society provides us with unexpected challenges which often arise from factors beyond our control. For example:

   In the crowded city, bustling with life. . .
   – many people are lonely and neglected. Why?
   – many people are isolated from their families and friends. Why?
   – even the basics of education seem to be taught differently. Why?

2. Consider yourself in regard to your children or the children whom you teach.

   What are their main interests?
   Can you share their preferences in music?
   How do they dress? (Can you think of yourself at the same age?)
   How do their interests in travel (?), money (?), employment (?) differ from your own?
   Can you list some reasons why their *choices* differ from yours?

3. In the following poem a Welsh modern poet, R. S. Thomas,

14

who is also a clergyman in charge of an ancient church in north-west Wales, reflects on the isolation of his church and on the absence of a congregation.

THE MOON IN LLEYN
The last quarter of the moon
of Jesus gives way
to the dark; the serpent
digests the egg. Here
on my knees in this stone
church, that is full only
of the silent congregation
of shadows and the sea's
sound, it is easy to believe
Yeats was right. Just as though
choirs had not sung, shells
have swallowed them; the tide laps
at the Bible; the bell fetches
no people to the brittle miracle
of the bread. The sand is waiting
for the running back of the grains
in the wall into its blond
glass. Religion is over, and
what will emerge from the body
of the new moon, no one
can say.
    But a voice sounds
in my ear: Why so fast,
mortal? These very seas
are baptized. The parish
has a saint's name time cannot
unfrock. In cities that
have outgrown their promise people
are becoming pilgrims
again, if not to this place,
then to the recreation of it
in their own spirits. You must remain
kneeling. Even as this moon
making its way through the earth's
cumbersome shadow, prayer, too,
has its phases.
    From *Laboratories of the Spirit* (Macmillan 1975).

What strikes you most about this poem?

HAS THE CHURCH A PLACE IN THE SUPERMARKET SOCIETY?

Traditionally, the Church has helped to provide some pattern and stability for many people's lives. It was the Church which provided ritual celebrations for the important sequence of events which, beginning with baptism, initiated children gradually into the sacramental life of the whole community, later giving public ratification to the public adult choices of marriage or priestly vocation, and finally giving meaning and purpose to death, the end of life. Such a sacramental system easily transcended the racial and cultural differences of diverse lands and languages. Associated with this social dimension of its work, was the Church's concern for education as well as for the care and supervision of young people at many stages of their growth from childhood to the society of which these practices became the fabric, for it helped to supply the basic direction for an understanding of the Christian meaning of life.

But so many church buildings, once filled with worshippers, are now empty, or, in R. S. Thomas' words,

> full only
> of the silent congregation
> of shadows.

For those who sigh for the old days, it is as if

> religion is over, and
> what will emerge from the body
> of the new moon,
> no one
> can say.

Can the church change?

This 'unchanging Roman Church', uniform in its Latin language, liturgical rites and church discipline for centuries, the same Church in every part of the world, was the only kind of Catholic Church known to most of us before the late 1950s and early 1960s. Somehow, this ability to remain unchanged seemed to be related to the God 'without shadow of change or alteration' who had commissioned his Son, Jesus Christ, to found the Church as his abiding presence on earth until the end of time, and who guaranteed to be with it at all times. There is no denying that many found this an important gut-level proof of God's fidelity towards his people. But there were too many historical instances where the Church seemed set against any form of advance, scientific or social, which it had not itself authorized. To return to the images of the concentric circles, the Church here appeared to be claiming a form of total control over every aspect of human life. It saw itself at the centre, and it commanded, directed, and taught at all levels to those within its circumference. Outside this Church, said some (in a very narrow interpretation of a famous traditional expression), there was no salvation. Mission sermons often stressed the experience of soldiers, who seeing their Catholic comrades die tranquilly after the visit of the chaplain, exclaimed that the Catholic religion was a hard one to live in, but a consoling one to die in. And it was. It is in no way to deny the strength of such a Church to suggest that some of its previous strengths were so in relation to the more limited possibilities of a very different kind of society. Changed circumstances now make many aspects of such a Church an anachronism, especially for the young who have never known it!

Perhaps there is an analogy with another powerful, all-controlling authority which once exercised a most remarkable influence over a great portion of the world – the British Empire. Up to the beginning of the Second World War, it was possible to look at a map of the world and see from the red shading the extent of the Empire 'on which the sun never sets'. It is doubtful whether very many of the former colonies wish to return to their former status; it is doubtful, too, whether very many people in Britain could justify the existence of the Empire today except in terms of the historical wealth and power which it once conferred. The reasonable success of the British Commonwealth suggests that there are some enduring ties beyond those of language and history, but few

17

people today would like to make a defence of colonialism in terms of its overriding benefits.

If we look at an earlier period of imperial expansion following the great discovery voyages of the fifteenth century, we see the flag of trade was often accompanied by the Christian cross. The justification for this was that the gospel was to be proclaimed to all nations. It is uncomfortable for us to realize that there were similar church justifications for slavery, especially at the time when the plantation system was introduced into the Americas. But this kind of historical hindsight only goes to point up how slowly and how gradually the Church has become aware of its mission. In an absolutist age, the Church knew its most powerful era of authority and privilege. In the imperial ages, the Church also organized and promoted missionary endeavour which inspired saintly men and women to try to bring the gospel to other races. The Church 'always in need of reform' of the Second Vatican Council set itself to be the Church of the modern world, a source of joy and hope (*Gaudium et Spes*) for that world.

Was it all Pope John's fault?

Twenty years after the first talk of an ecumenical Council, we can better appreciate its dynamic aspect. The Council was first of all a movement before it became an event. Secondly, as an event it lasted much longer than anticipated, precisely because of the complexity of the issues. Thirdly, the collegiality (including re-spect for the diversity as well as for the uniformity of opinion within the Church) has been enshrined into a continuing review of major questions of the Church's life which has seen a succession of Synods, preparations through consultation of the Church prior to the Synods and the documentation and directions arising from the Synods themselves. One thing seems certain: the Church has not exchanged one pre-set position for another. The changing Church seems here to stay. Where there have been reaffirmations of a traditional position (e.g. *Humanae Vitae* in 1968) there are still many people claiming to be loyal to the Church who believe that there are other approaches to be considered to the traditional questions of marriage and procreation. For instance, the National Pastoral Congress in Liverpool in 1980 resolved that:

the Church's teaching on marriage can develop only through a fundamental re-examination of the teaching on marriage, on sexuality and on contraception.

a. Such re-examination should leave open the possibility of change and development in the Church's teaching on marriage, on sexuality and on contraception.

b. Indeed there is now a need for change and development in this teaching.

(The Tablet)

Today's Church needs many centres

The Church has undergone a major transformation in the past fifteen to twenty years. At the same time, the rate of renewal (or even of the more limited *adaptation*) has not been uniform even in the same country. How much more striking, then, seem some of the differences when our greater ability to travel and to make armchair journeys in front of the television, allow us to encounter a Church very different from the one we have known. I would like to suggest, then, that one way of appreciating the demands made on us as members of the Church in this period of rapid transition may be to spell out in detail some of the strengths of the 'circle' Church which may need to find new forms of expression in our many-centred society. Setting out these contrasts in opposition to each other oversimplifies the issues and runs the further risk of appearing to set up a commendable position against one no longer tenable. But recognizing this difficulty can help us to remember that the move towards diversity and pluralism has also to include respect for viewpoints and attitudes long associated with the tradition of the Church in a particular country or locality. We need to be reminded as well that our young people have never personally experienced the 'circle' Church of the following comparison table.

Some contrasts between the 'circle' and the 'many-centred' Church

Aspect	'Circle' Church	Many-centred Church
P A R I S H	The parish, centre of the village or section of a town, with its 'control' of the year through its feasts, its general regulation of time through its bells, its 'supervision' of the lives of the people through its priests, its ability to form a close-knit community, proud of its own achievements, an unchanging hierarchy of age and position.	In a society of apartments and of marked social and physical mobility, there is no longer the same stable community. The absence of a deep sense of 'belonging' and the common identity conferred by the Catholic 'sub-culture' encourages people to seek less stable communities (pubs and clubs); they 'shop around' looking for places and people which satisfy their spiritual needs as felt in today's world and culture.
A U T H O R I T Y	The priest, through his superior education and accepted role in the group, his local knowledge and close links with his people, was one of the main strengths of the Church. The parish primary school, taught by some religious, conferred a social place and role which influenced the whole community. Both stability and some social mobility were promoted by the school which was also the 'social' centre for many parish activities. Authority of parents was reinforced by clergy and teachers.	Ever broadening education is open to all, thereby promoting mobility in various forms. Secondary and tertiary education become more common and take people away from the local area. The 'pluralism' of life challenges the stability, traditional language and selectivity of a theology capable of being expressed only in the language and thought forms of an earlier age. Laity, encouraged to take a more active part in terms of their own competences, often find themselves in conflict with the exercise of authority which takes no account of their experiences as adults and parents.

Aspect	'Circle' Church	Many-centred Church
C O M M U N I C A T I O N	Information often mediated by the authority of the printed word and the statements of authority figures (parents, pastors, teachers) was thereby 'controlled'. Forms of real control and censorship of ideas were always possible.	Our many sources of information present us with an average of 1700 daily 'messages'. This information is often 'raw' and accessible to all at the same time without any screening or censorship.
M O R A L I T Y	The village, town and/or sub-culture exerted a strong pressure towards a moral conformity and to upholding conventional standards. It provided good modelling behaviour for people at all stages of life in what was a 'predictable' and unchanging path.	The anonymity of the city and the social and physical mobility today give access to other places and other possibilities. Social and moral standards become in fact much more the responsibility of the individual. Other ways of behaving are constantly projected through the media; the world seems to be in a process of constant change.

What does it all mean for us?

This kind of comparison table first of all shows up the far-reaching effects of social change. Once successful institutions, such as the parish, have difficulty in meeting the needs of a new society, so different from the medieval one in which parishes came into being. It is not to question either the basic aim or the historical achievements of such institutions, but to wonder about their continuing relevance in a different kind of society. Parishes seem to need the kind of renewal which is thorough enough to change many things which have already passed into history. Thus, for example, we could consider the former role of sodalities in parish life, or Sunday Vespers, or processions. All of these provided a social setting, spoke to a certain ideal, and promoted the comfortable aspects of things done together such as the singing of hymns, the saying of familiar prayers, the devotions expressed through novenas. Everything took place under the benign approval, supervision and control of the parish priest. Now, in all churches, Sunday evenings have become a difficult time to organize anything religious in the parish, especially given the powerful attractions of TV stations, themselves offering religious programmes which may appeal to a wide range of religious interests. The long-running success of programmes such as 'Songs of Praise' may be explained by interest in good hymns well sung or by satisfaction in being able to participate even vicariously in ecumenical services. Many viewers expressed deep interest in programmes such as 'The Long Search'. What we are seeing here is that it is not only the loss of some traditional supports which is responsible for the decline of the parish in the many-centred Church. There is also the expanded horizon of interests which brings forward other religious and human questions extending far beyond the former scope of the parish. Even when we use the word 'ecumenical' we are using a Greek word which has the sense of 'everywhere' and not simply our own corner of the world. We live, according to McCluhan's image, in the 'global village'.

Even our use of space and time has changed. . .

A second effect of looking at the comparison chart may be to long for the security of things of the past that seemed never to change. This kind of 'dream' can be nostalgic and utopian but also unrealistic. Perhaps there is something about this aspiration in itself which is in some way connected with our being human. Our ways of looking at those fundamental anthropological categories, *space* and *time*, is very important here, for these are the criteria which show the greatest differences between the 'circle' Church and the many-centred Church. There is an important sense in which one of the main 'effects' of the first document of Vatican II, the liturgical constitution, has been to change our way of using the *space* of the church and the *time* we spend there. Thus, for example, the renewed attention to the Scriptures, read in the vernacular in the believing assembly, has changed the emphasis experienced by generations during the Latin Mass. One very important change is that the word is now *heard*, not simply read in a missal while the priest reads it in Latin, and another is the restoration of the homily (in place of the more formal 'sermon') as a reflection on the texts read. The sequence of readings through the liturgical cycle of the Church re-presents for us each year that sequence of events in time and space which marked out God's covenant with the Jews and the life of his Son Jesus and the Church he founded. This is constant even in the cycle of change, that is to say, the celebration of the common memory of those events which bind believers together. This celebration of this memorial ('Do this in memory of me') is so important that it is the reason for the existence of the parish itself. If to ensure this celebration, traditional structures have to be replaced (and this may include sodalities, novenas, devotions which were important in another time and in a different society) then this may be the price to be paid for ensuring a contemporary relevance which may make it possible for the young to feel that they are welcome in such a church.

What some of the young do tell us, however, is far from comforting. For many, Mass is still 'dead boring' because 'the priest raves on and on'. The girls who said this were talking of the 'new' liturgy, not the old!

That is why the concerns of the young, their attitude and conduct towards the church they see, are such important things to be recognized and reflected on by the whole Church. Sometimes the only reason why we insist that certain things be done or not done, is by an appeal to our authority as parents, teachers or simply adults. However adequate this may be with young children, it can be opposed to that ideal of education which sees the importance of helping to guide the young towards an ever-expanding autonomy. It may be worth taking a closer look at the young people who present their elders with so many challenges, especially if we recall Margaret Mead's contention that our modern society presents us with the new challenges that 'these are the two generations – pioneers in a new era and their children, who have as yet to find a way of communicating about the world in which both live, though their perceptions of it are so different.'[1]

[1] Op. cit., p. 110.

'Five Cries of Youth'

In 1974, Merton P. Strommen published the results of a highly complex study of young people in the United States, called *Church Youth*. With the help of his associates, he prepared a 420-item survey which was then administered to a large group of young people, in fact over 7000 of them. The framework in which he finally presented his work was that entitled 'Five Cries of Youth', or 'Anguishes' of youth. Allowing for the marked cultural differences between the United States and other countries, I think there is value in considering the patterns he discerned.

The first was 'the cry of self hatred'. This was the general title for such things as a sense of worthlessness, self-criticism, loneliness, anxiety about faith, poor and immature personal relationships, academic problems, family disunity and so on.

A second cry was that 'of the psychological orphan'. This was the general term to describe the anguish of those who live in an atmosphere of parental hatred and distrust, arising from things such as family discord, lack of family social concern, the gap between youth and parents, the competitive appeals from outside the family.

The third cry was that of 'social protest'. By this expression, the researchers tried to describe the criticism of adults made by young people when they accused adults of not caring about them, of the desire of the young for change, of their feeling for people and their social concern.

A fourth cry was that 'of the prejudiced'. This seemed to arise from the pressure to accept and live by stereotypes and prejudgements, to conform, to accept racism and various forms of discrimination.

It may come as some reassurance to adults to learn that the fifth cry was 'the cry of the joyous'. This description ranged over a wide number of things associated with happiness, but was particularly relevant to quiet exuberance over the simple pleasures of being alive.

It is striking that these five cries are addressed in a particular way to issues which were once the traditional province of the Church. If the young do not find reassurance and help in the Church to cope with these difficulties, the problems still persist and there is an unrelenting search for solutions. Some of these are sadly inadequate, as studies of drug-taking and alcoholism among young people show only too starkly. Perhaps one way of seeing the role of the Church in the pluralist society might be to see what kinds of services could be offered (and by whom) to help to respond to the needs of the young.

The absence of the young people from much of the celebration of liturgy, or an attempt to control their expression through the hymns and the music they like to use, is a serious matter for the whole Church. The different generations within the Church need one another. John H. Westerhoff in his book, *Will our children have faith?*, speaks of the importance of the generations of 'memory', those of the elderly and of 'the present' (adults), and of the generation of 'hope' (the young), finding ways of being of service to one another. This is the natural way in which there can be formed a community of different generations from which all would benefit. But there is a warning to be issued here.

Dynamic faith or static religion?

One obvious result of rapid change, of generation gaps, of marked differences of opinion within the Church, is that the uniformity of belief and practice which marked religion in a more stable age is no longer present. 'Religion is over', says the poet. The key word here is the word 'religion'. When we use an expression such as 'religious practice', we are referring to one of the most important functions of religion, namely, the practices, rituals, patterns of living which are most characteristic of the regular functioning of a religion. In the Catholic sub-culture, this aspect was so important that it was the usual norm for evaluating a member of the Catholic community. One of the questions regularly asked by the priest engaged in parish visitation was, 'Are you practising Catholics?'. In a negative context, ordinary language description of non-practising Catholics often made use of the word 'faith', as in the phrase describing someone no longer attending Mass or the church: 'He's lost *the* faith.' The definite article 'the' here is quite important. What is being said is that this person no longer attends church or is associated with the religious practices of that particular group who hold '*the* faith' together. There is a sense in which this use of the word 'faith' is more of a sociological description than a theological one.

Faith has always been appreciated within the Christian tradition as 'gift of God' (*donum Dei*) given freely by a bountiful God. The association of those baptized within the same Church naturally confers certain common benefits and finds certain common expressions. No one is perfect in hope nor in charity; none of us are perfect in faith. But we do have the firm assurance that when we stand together and affirm together what was once affirmed by others at the time of our baptism, or what was the formula devised by our ancestors in the faith at a particular moment of crisis, we are saying more than any one of us can say with assurance by himself. 'It is in this important sense that we can say that "personal" faith needs the support of the believing community of faith, those who profess "the faith".'

A second and indispensable condition for describing faith is that, as 'free gift', it is offered in freedom and grows most naturally under conditions which respect the freedom of the recipient. This issue is central to any discussion of faith and will be taken up in more detail in a later section. Faith needs to be lived out 'in the freedom with which Christ made us free', in the 'glorious liberty of the children of God'. It is in this sense, too, that we can see that personal and communitarian faith finds forms of expression through the practices of religion. In this sense, faith needs the support and complementarity of religion for its full expression within a community.

But the reverse is not necessarily true. The practices of religion may be the result of habit, of nationality, of prejudice or of social conformity and may be marked more by convention and sameness than by anything dynamic. In the name of religion, some of the finest things have been done throughout history. Unfortunately, we could also say that religion has been given as the justification for duplicity, persecutions, the burning of heretics, forced conversions and so on.

In a time of rapid social and cultural change, the dissatisfaction of the young with the formal practices of religion is a well-known and widespread occurrence. This is naturally upsetting for parents and teachers, who may see the young person rejecting something which they esteem and which they judge useful for others too. Perhaps, however, it needs to be said that the stage of rejection of religious practice may be more of a cultural pointer than anything more radical. The associations of formal religious services with certain kinds of buildings, dress, posture, behaviour, music and attention, may be so distant in cultural terms that the young people are not so much rejecting God as rather a whole way of behaving which no longer makes sense to them. It has often been observed by those close to the young that teenagers are rejecting 'churchianity' rather than 'Christianity', the Church rather than the person of Jesus. Whether we call this a 'crisis of faith' or a

26

'loss of faith' is something to be looked at in a later section. It certainly is a rejection of religion. But that rejection, in itself, may sometimes be necessary if the young person is to become emancipated from an image of God and his service which has never developed beyond the cultural conditioning of a family, church or society.

The euphoria which followed the Second Vatican Council produced notable signs of new growth in the Church. It did not, however, solve all the problems. Perhaps it is important for the whole Church to recognize the questioning of each successive generation as an important reminder that people are graced individually by faith, and not saved in spite of themselves by the practices of religion. The Church 'always in need of reform' has always to face (and to heed as well!) the searching questions of its newer members who often see it, disconcertingly for us elders, as locked into cultural forms which no longer meet the needs of a complex modern society.

For personal reflection and group discussion

1. What has been said in the preceding section is true not just for the English-speaking Church. A young Frenchman writes:

God
are you sure that your church can still celebrate?
This morning
I found her looking tired and drawn
haggard and grey.
And still those long, boring sermons.
Old lady,
every Sunday,
she powders her face, puts on her make-up for the occasion,
but her lipstick looks ugly,
and under her faded hat she looks sadder than ever.
God
tell me. . .
Are you really counting on this old lady to invite
young people to dance?
God
it's time to bring this dead celebration to life.
Not like it was in the old days

rummaging through drawers stuffed with memories,
but a celebration of the future.
Risen from the dead!

(Jean Debruyne, 1000 Guitares pour Dieu,
Tarbes 18–21 July 1981)

2. A young Australian remarks, less poetically no doubt, but with a similar strength of feeling:

When I was young, I was drilled into believing in God, so now I tend to go against him. . . . I wish the Church would teach the children of tomorrow in a different way than I was taught. What do I want from the Church? I don't know. Usually I think of the Church as something away from me, something that's just there. I'll tell you what I want! Fun! – in that I can go to a rock Mass and have a ball, in that I can enjoy the celebration of the meal with Christ – do it in happiness and total fulfilment.

3. Can you relate any of the above comments to 'The Five Cries of Youth'?

4. David Lodge's novel *How far can you go?* (Penguin 1981) is a witty and sensitive novel, highly relevant to the issues ex- plored in this book. Its opening chapter, 'How it was', presents a group of young English Catholic students attending early morning Mass on St Valentine's day in 1952. The novel pro- ceeds to trace the personal development, relationships and struggles of each member of the group in the context of the changing church and society of the next three tumultuous decades.

You may like to read Lodge's novel in the light of our first two chapters. Do you see anything of yourself and your friends in his characters?

3

GROWING *INTO* FAITH?

It is a central contention of this book that one of the main emphases of our work as parents and teachers with young people in our rapidly changing society is that of trying to help them grow *into* faith. We once could have said with some accuracy in a more stable society 'grow *in* faith'. In this description, faith was seen as a gift of God conferred through baptism. Our programmes of preparation for first confession and first communion (even the order of reception was an important theological statement in itself!) were intended to lead to greater knowledge and understanding through the instruction received, and so have the young people better disposed to receive the grace of the sacraments. Not many years later, sometimes at ten years of age, confirmation was conferred, usually in the presence of parents or sponsors at least, and a strong emphasis was given to the importance of remaining steadfast in the faith, 'strong and perfect Christians' as the catechism put it. This was a system with a strong community dimension. It had the benefit of some centuries of tradition, and it was generally supported by the encouragement and example of some adult members of the community. Rapid cultural change, however, makes such a progression one limiting choice among many others. Neither fidelity nor perseverance are necessarily attractive virtues to young people growing up in the many-choice, supermarket society where they are faced with so many alternative philosophies and life-styles.

Growing *into* faith, it has already been said, is to place less emphasis on 'keeping' or 'preserving' something which is static, and much more on responding to the continuing call of the God whom we meet at different stages of our lives – and not merely within the confines of one particular institution or system. Growing *into* faith puts more emphasis first on the importance of appreciating faith as something dynamic, that is, something subject to the laws of growth and change, a challenge which is God's call inviting a free response. While faith is, in a chronological sense at least, a 'community' faith acquired, learned, and appreciated within the home, school and parish, it is this very 'community' which is often rejected or reappraised critically by many adolescents as they come to realize other choices open to them. There is no uniform pattern to this. In the 1979 Symposium of European Bishops, gathered to discuss the question of the faith of young people, Monsignor Klaus Hammerle, Bishop of Aix-La-Chapelle, suggested some of the most commonly advanced reasons for difficulties in faith experienced by the young. There is a wide range of differing reasons offered as to why 'faith is made to appear strange and difficult':

The situation of the faith of young people today does not mean only where young people are with regard to the faith, but equally where the faith is as regards young people.

Faith is outside their experience.

The absolute demands and the exclusive finality of the Christian message easily make young people suspicious of a Christianity seen as an ideology, or something put forward as a fanaticism.

Dogmas, obligatory standards, the Institutional Church, are all in sharp contrast when we are talking about a dynamic freedom with young people.

Christian faith, founded on an historical event two thousand years ago and passed on through historical tradition, can be neither understood nor provoke any interest with the young.

Their limited experiences of human living, especially imperfection and death, mingle in such a way as to make them see life as having possibilities other than those only in Christianity.

The actual appearance of Christianity and the Church no longer appears credible to the young.

Fourteen years previously, the final version of the 'Church in the Modern World' (Par. 7, p. 907 Flannery) noted:

A change in attitudes and structures frequently calls accepted values into question. This is true above all of young people who have grown impatient at times and indeed rebellious in their distress. Conscious of their own importance in the life of society, they aspire to play their part in it all the sooner.

30

Ten years after this paragraph, Pope Paul VI in *Evangelization Today* takes up the same theme saying:

> Existing circumstances suggest to us that we should devote our attention in particular to young people. Their increasing numbers, the fact that they are making their presence felt in society, the questions which trouble them should arouse in everyone the desire to offer them zealously and wisely, the evangelical ideal as something to be known and lived.
>
> (EN no. 72)

In October 1979, Pope John Paul II wrote in *Catechesi Tradendae* no. 25:

> Thus through catechesis the gospel kerygma (the initial ardent proclamation by which a person is one day overwhelmed and brought to the decision to entrust himself to Jesus Christ by faith) is gradually deepened, developed in its implicit consequences, explained in language that includes an appeal to reason, and channelled towards Christian practice in the Church and the world. . . . The truths studied in catechesis are the same truths that touched the person's heart when he heard them for the first time.

This well known distancing from the cultural aspects of religion (*the* faith), which is so marked in these quotations, suggests that faith has not simply to be preserved but rather chosen (or even re-chosen) freely at different moments of life. A childhood faith will not suffice to meet the demands of being an adult. Speaking not of theological faith but simply of 'faith' in the decisions made by governments in modern societies, Margaret Mead suggests why there is what she calls a 'crisis of faith' in today's world:

> Men . . . feel they have been deprived of every kind of security. I believe that this crisis in faith can be attributed, at least in part, to the fact that there are now no elders who know more than the young themselves about what the young are experiencing.
>
> (Culture and Commitment, p. 105)

For many of us, these young people have names and faces and personal histories, and we, who are their parents and teachers, are dealing not with a *problem*, but with a person. Consider the following letter written by Pascale, a sixteen year old girl from Lille in France, in response to a request from the animator of a discussion group at school:

31

HOW PASCALE WAS DECEIVED[1]

I went to Mass this morning. For me, that was really something, because I never go. I had no intention of going beforehand. It was only when I woke up at 7.20 to the ringing of the church bells that I decided to go to the 7.30 Mass. Why? I don't go any more, because the last experience I had of Mass was a bad one. I had kept this memory of something quite grim with a continual 'blah blah'.

But I told myself that perhaps I had a wrong idea of it and it would cost me nothing to try it again. I went there also in memory of an old man who died last year and who was a kind of grandfather for me.

The fact that this was a village Mass perhaps exaggerates things a bit, but I am going to try to tell you just what I saw and heard.

I was really sickened, disgusted right from the first minute. The priest came into the sanctuary, said a sentence so quickly that the people tried to repeat it just as quickly, said something else they repeated, and so on like that several times, simply, stupidly. The first metaphor that came to my mind (exaggerated, I know) was that of a billy goat leading a flock of sheep. If the goat 'baas' they all go 'Baa!' If the goat goes off, they all follow him. If he gives an order, they are all on their feet to obey.

It was there I became aware of the enormous difference between what was done in that little church and Catholicism. I was sorry for these people who were there, who needed a guide in their lives, but who took the one given them instead of looking for one themselves.

They knew the whole Mass by heart and said it like good pupils reciting a lesson they had learned, always the same, something they repeat and are made to repeat every time they go to Mass. And they go out from there happy to think they are going forward to their Saviour while all they're doing is 'marking time'. How can you build a house if you always put down the same stone?

I think this is the last time I am going to Mass. I had gone there with some hope, the hope of discovering something, of finding out I had made a mistake, but all I found there was one huge fraud. I was back in primary school again. The teacher was saying the lesson sentence by sentence and the pupils were all

[1] Translated from *Des Lycéens De Second Cycle Disent Leur Foi'* (Secrétariat National De L'Aumonerie de L'Enseignement Public 1979), p. 12.

repeating it as best they could while trying not to look at their books. There comes back to me one detail which amused me: perhaps I understood it wrongly but it struck me. Two old ladies were standing side by side. One of them was reciting the 'Our Father' without any help while the other was looking at her missal. The one who did not have her book open was looking at the other with a superior air. The latter closed her missal quickly and continued her recitation while giving her neighbour a sly look. I had the impression they were saying:

'Now then, Granny, you have not been taught your lesson properly?'

'Ah, yes, but see I am reciting it quite as well as you are. I was just pretending a moment ago!'

Other things had already struck me. We are often told: 'The church is open to all. The Lord receives all his brethren.' Why then do we find the door closed if ever you want to go into a church outside of Mass time? Why do they take up a collection in certain churches without even telling you for whose benefit it is intended?

In searching and reflecting you can find some anomalies. I believe you can find anomalies in everything dished out to us, but not in the things we do for ourselves since we do them according to our ideas and tastes. Everyone has to find his own path, his own life, his own purpose all by himself.

Pascale is a voluntary member of a Catholic discussion group looking at '*the* faith' from outside. She is like a member of an audience looking at a play in which she feels no involvement. Yet she seems to be a baptized Christian who has received the gift of faith in a formal sense at least. She admits that her general distaste for the Mass may not have been altogether fair, and so is prepared 'to try it again'. In the absence of a welcome and of personal involvement in the community, she now seems further away than before. Many of us have met Pascale and we know what she is saying. We will return to this point in a later section, but let us use this same example to see what are some of the observable characteristics of this dynamic gift called faith.

One of the most enduring ways of talking about faith in different religious traditions is that of the journey or pilgrimage of faith, so strongly revived in our times by Vatican II's description of our Church as a 'pilgrim people'. Sometimes there is a too easy assumption that questions of loss of faith, or of doubt or of diffi-

33

culties with certain religious rules or practices are mainly problems of young people. Nothing could be further from the truth taught us by experience and by the nature of faith itself, which both show us that we are challenged by faith many times in our lives. There is certainly a challenge to faith presented in a time of persecution or discrimination when our response might be best described as 'holding on to the faith' or 'preserving the faith'; i.e. despite the difficulties, with no certainty as to what our holding on to the faith may call us to do or to suffer, we respond in faith. In a time of marked religious apathy such as we seem to have lived through recently ('Modern man does not so much deny God as ignore him', suggested Pope Paul VI in *Evangelization Today*), sitting back waiting for the occasion to defend the faith would seem to be the opposite of living by faith.

The image of the journey, the pilgrimage, the implied ups and downs which are so familiar to us through our experience of living, all give a special importance, I feel, to recent studies which provide us with a framework to look at this development of faith through discernible steps or stages.

Some recognizable stages of faith?

'Conversion to faith', writes Karl Rahner, 'is always a process with many stages and these need not necessarily follow the same course in every individual. . . . Faith is never awakened by someone having something communicated to him purely from outside, addressed solely to his naked understanding as such. To lead to faith is always to assist understanding of what has already been experienced in the depth of human reality as grace'[2]

When James W. Fowler, a young Methodist minister in the United States, had to spend a year working with experienced ministers following a special year of pastoral training, he began to perceive some kind of pattern in the more than two hundred interviews he conducted which invited people to tell their own story of their pilgrimage in faith. Reflecting on these stories with the help of certain key ideas gleaned mainly from the psychologist Erik Erikson (life as a series of stages, each of which has to be negotiated successfully for continuing growth), Fowler began to see that this idea of stage-development as formulated by Piaget, Erikson and Kohlberg, did have many applications in trying to

[2] *Encyclopedia of Theology* (Burns & Oates 1975), article on 'Faith'.

speak about the 'framework' or 'manifestations' of faith, if not always about its content. A structural development theory states that the human mind has certain formal structures within which development takes place under the influence of a certain social environment. Progress to another stage depends on the successful achievement of the preceding one. Stages are not necessarily 'better' than the preceding one: but they are obviously and observably different. Fowler uses the analogy of a series of lenses to try to express the differences between stages. With one lens, the object is observable and can be seen in totality. A more powerful lens reveals things that were always there but not capable of being observed. A continuing series of such lenses will present more and more detail. But the whole was in a sense complete even in the first viewing.

Fowler's work is a long-term study, and in his published books and articles he stresses that his general theoretical framework needs to be consolidated by a much wider range of practical studies. In general, however, his work has been welcomed by a large number of theologians and pastoral workers as being true to their experience. One such writer, John H. Westerhoff, has formulated a similar way of approaching the question of faith in a pastoral context, and reference will be made to the insights of both Fowler and Westerhoff. In case it may be thought that all of this emphasis is somehow outside any discussion of religious faith, we can show how the general idea of faith development can be found in the theology of Friedrich von Hügel in *The Mystical Elements of Religion*, published in 1927.

It will be difficult in a short space to include all the important insights of Fowler or the practical applications suggested by Westerhoff. Fowler's work, in particular, includes insights from both psychology and theology, and this has led him, in the interests of clarity, to formulate a special terminology and language which may seem very off-putting to the non-specialist. The following presentation, therefore, attempts to set out the main insights without too much reliance on exclusively technical language. Fowler's work is a good example of the way in which the development of knowledge, so much emphasized in earlier sections, challenges us.

Faith of childhood and family

In families that are traditionally Christian in their beliefs and ways of living, faith is *experienced* by the child within the family itself

35

and in the institutions favoured and supported by it. Westerhoff calls the first stage of faith 'experienced'. Fowler uses the technical term 'intuitive-projective', because things which are *intuitive* in the child, such as forms of loyalty and pride in one's name and family, find some kind of expression or *projection* in the family as well as in the immediate surroundings of the family. It is obvious that the example of parents and immediate family is a strong influence either in a positive or negative way.

Around the seventh year, there appears to be a second stage of this childhood faith. Traditionally, this has been called the 'age of reason' and it has been the usual age at which children have been initiated into the sacraments of penance and Eucharist in recent years, because it has been considered that by this time, most children can distinguish between the special character of Christian sacraments and other customs of which they have had some experience. It is because of this initiation into some of the accepted practices of the community that Westerhoff calls this stage the 'affiliative', that is, the stage of accepting 'sonship' or 'daughter-ship' within the family. Fowler's expression, 'mythic-literal', attempts to include two complementary aspects: the child is introduced into the main stories (myths) of the group, but is capable of understanding them only in a fairly literal way. In a general way, this stage seems to last until around the eleventh or twelfth year. Von Hügel uses the expression 'institutional' to include the way in which most children come to inherit the faith of their family through the *institution* of the family, church and school.

If we express these ideas of childhood faith on the one diagram it would look like this:

CHILDHOOD FAITH

FOWLER	WESTERHOFF	VON HÜGEL
INTUITIVE – PROJECTIVE MYTHIC – LITERAL	EXPERIENCED AFFILIATIVE	INSTITUTIONAL

It should be pointed out that for most children raised in a stable family, this is a kind of 'apprenticeship' to the practices associated with the manifestation of faith through religious observances. It is, to use another word much used by educators, a process of 'socialization' into religion. It is central to our discussion so far to remember that this kind of process appears to have been successful in a more stable society, especially before the extension of formal schooling introduced the new element of a prolonged adolescence in which the assumption of a more complete autonomy and responsibility was necessarily deferred until the demands of secondary (and increasingly, tertiary) education had been met.

'Critical', 'searching' and 'individuative–reflexive' faith

We can all confirm from our own experience that faith grows beyond the boundaries imposed on it by childhood. This is true for any general sense in which we use the word 'faith', so that there is necessarily a loss of what Fowler calls a *'synthetic'* world-view which once included Santa Claus, Snow White and the fairies at the bottom of the garden with the same certainty as God, angels and saints. It seems important to note this, because it may help us to see this 'critical' or 'searching' stage as a natural and necessary movement towards the development of a more mature, personal faith – without which *synthetic-conventional* (or conformist) faith (Fowler's third stage), dependent on our unquestioning acceptance of institutional authority, can easily become a permanent home.

In the more precise Christian sense of faith as 'belief in God who is Creator, Redeemer and Sanctifier', we may have to remind ourselves that despite the Church and the sacramental system, our progress towards God in faith is not a uniform ascent throughout life but a path marked by falls, struggles, repentances, and new beginnings. Some negative theologies of recent centuries have made it hard for us to realize that these struggles are related to the nature of faith itself and to its essentially dynamic character. We do need to keep this perspective in mind when we encounter the questions, doubts and searchings of Pascale and her peers.

If the words 'critical' and 'searching' are sufficiently clear, it is important to see what more is being suggested by Fowler's 'individuative–reflexive' faith. The terminology here marks out the important transition from a faith accepted from others on their authority, to the beginnings of a faith which is more independently chosen and supported by personal conviction. Of course, what is being indicated here is the beginning of what may be a life-long process. The word 'individuative' reminds us of the typical adolescent movement towards self-acceptance, a growing sense of identity as a young adult with the potentialities of an adult, while the word 'reflexive' suggests that there is less uncritical acceptance of the ideas of others, and more attention to personal opinions. Fowler suggests that this stage *may* begin in mid or late adolescence, but may not occur for some until a personal crisis in later life shatters unquestioning conformism. Diagrammatically, the stage could be represented as follows:

ADOLESCENT FAITH

FOWLER	WESTERHOFF	VON HÜGEL
from SYNTHETIC–CONVENTIONAL to INDIVIDUATIVE–REFLEXIVE	from AFFILIATIVE to SEARCHING	from INSTITUTIONAL to CRITICAL

Teachers in a secondary school, parents with teenage children, meet young people at just this stage.

It is at this stage during adolescence that many of us encounter the young people with whom we are most concerned, and often, despite our own experience, we take this searching, critical attitude as signifying loss or lack of faith when in reality it seems to be the transition point between the faith of childhood and the beginnings of a more adult faith. It is for this reason well described by many authors as a 'crisis of faith' precisely because it is a turning *away* which may also lead to a turning *towards*. The tentative nature of such a movement is well marked in the following passage from Pope Paul VI's letter on *Evangelization Today*:

> It is evident that the circumstances of our time make it ever more urgent to provide catechetical instruction under some form of catechumenate for the many adolescents who, under the influence of grace, are gradually discerning the countenance of Christ and are beginning to appreciate the necessity of surrendering themselves to him.

(EN 44)

The provisional and dynamic qualities of this quest are strikingly illustrated in the words 'gradually discerning' and 'beginning to appreciate'.

As we are older people, our relationship with the young is necessarily marked by the degree and style of authority we exercise in their regard. Now, as we have noted, it is precisely this role of authority which is one of the distinguishing points between different stages of faith according to the authors we are here

38

citing. If faith is to become critical, searching and more personal, nothing can be a greater obstacle than apparently well-intentioned parents or teachers who try to ensure that this does not happen. In an address given under the title 'Freedom for Mission', Gerard W. Hughes, SJ, speaks strongly about this when he says:

> In religion the temptation is to remain one of the mis-called 'simple faithful'. It is good to be simple faithful but the term is misused. The temptation is to remain one of the simple faithful, meaning by that, credulous, unquestioning, docile and secure, opposed to any form of questioning which could jeopardize this security. . . . But the most effective way of destroying faith in ourselves and in others, especially the young, is to misuse words like loyalty, obedience and docility so that they serve the opposite purpose. They do not bring us to God: they block us from him. Instead of leading us to God, they hold us back in the infancy stage, stunting and stifling our growth. Such a religious attitude is a constant temptation for those who hold posts of responsibility in the institutional Church, and that includes all teachers and all parents.

> (Ms of unpublished address)

For the young person, C. Day Lewis reminds us, 'selfhood begins with a walking away': for the adult, 'love is proved in the letting go'. Didier Piveteau remarks that 'many Christian parents judge that one of the tasks of faith is to protect their children from the difficulties of doubt, from the separation brought about by the loss of the absolute and universal agreement. Such a catechesis is directed towards acquiring some kind of guarantee for the future.' (*Comment ouvrir les jeunes à la foi?*, p. 33)

At the same time, 'critical appraisal' and 'searching faith' which mark the end of childhood certainties do not of themselves lead to adult faith, nor do the young people themselves undergoing this change necessarily reassure us by their words and actions that they are enjoying their transition, or indeed, that they have any sense of 'going somewhere'. When a previously dutiful and happy child becomes apparently morose, secretive about his own affairs and openly hostile to normal standards of conduct and behaviour within the family, this can be seen by parents (and by teachers in analagous circumstances) as challenging the values of an order which is regarded as important. I think the elements of an answer to this problem can be found by considering the later stages of faith development according to the authors we are considering.

Towards an adult faith

Westerhoff sees the 'searching' stage being resolved for some people by another stage which he calls 'owned' faith. His meaning is not so much that someone possesses his 'own' faith, but rather that the person is *'owned'* or directed or controlled by a faith which gives direction to his life. This is not for Westerhoff simply one transition during life. He suggests, and I expect the experience of many adults would confirm, that this kind of 'conversion' is not always spectacular and lasting, but something glimpsed as a kind of vision of great clarity at certain moments of life, but re-chosen again and again at further moments of conversion until it can be said that one is indeed 'owned' by one's faith. It is in this sense that we must read Westerhoff as writing of stages of 'experiencing' and being 'affiliated' and becoming 'searchers' of a faith which comes at times to 'own' us: but the basic pattern will be repeated many times throughout life. I expect that one such moment of call to deeper faith must come to many adults, especially parents, when they encounter the searching and possible rejection of faith by young people. It is common enough to hear the anguish of parents behind words like, 'Where did we go wrong?', but it is not always perceived that this is a moment of 'crisis of faith' for both parents and children.

Fowler's fourth stage ('individuative–reflexive') is, as already explained, a movement towards something much more personal. It is often necessarily marked by distancing if not separation from what were once accepted norms of home and family. The general move towards a more marked autonomy, the only possible way for the young person to come towards that stage of self-direction implied by the idea of autonomy, is especially demanding if adults in positions of authority refuse to modify their own demands. Much more dialogue is called for, as well as the leaving of enough space for the young person to take responsibility for his own decisions (and their consequences!). This is especially true in allowing the young person to attempt to carry out some of the lofty ideal projects which arouse his enthusiasm at this age and stage.

It is important to recall here that Fowler, along with other theorists on stage development (e.g. Piaget, Kohlberg), is not proposing successive stages as necessarily 'better' than the ones that precede them. As already suggested, he finds his most apt comparison in that of lenses of increasing strength, each one of which looks at the same object but can give greater detail to what has been already seen. His two remaining stages of faith, however, are more finely nuanced than the 'mystical' as proposed by von Hügel, or the 'owned' of Westerhoff.

Stage 5, called 'paradoxical–consolidative', 'requires', says Fowler, 'a critical coming to terms with one's social unconscious: the myths, norms, ideal images, and prejudices built deeply into the self-system by virtue of one's upbringing within a particular social class, religious tradition, regional outlook, ethnic identity, national, community, or the like.' (*Life Maps: Conversations on the Journey of Faith* [Word Book Publishers, Waco, Texas, 1978]) There appear to be two movements here. The first is an appraisal of various influences which have affected a person's religious outlook – cultural prejudices arising from family, religion, ethnic background and nationality, and its expression through various cultural forms. A second movement is that of measuring self and personal history against the broader norm of what it is to be a complete human being. It is the perception and acceptance of limitations in oneself which need to be overcome so as to become more fully human. This explains the term *'paradoxical consolidative'*, though Fowler now prefers to use the term *'conjunctive faith'*.

Fowler's sixth stage indicates the possible limits of the preceding stage, and at the same time invites to even deeper perceptions of faith. The title, 'universalizing faith', describes a faith marked by 'an integration of life in faith in which immediacy of participation in the ultimate is the fruit of development, of discipline, and, likely, of genius'. ('Stages in Faith', a report to a symposium at Fordham University, September, 1975) Fowler admits that in his many attempts to describe this final stage he has been accused of 'uttering poetry'. We do seem to recognize this stage, however, in certain outstanding people such as the Mother Teresas, the Gandhis, the Dag Hammarsjkölds of this world – those inspiring people for whom we use the word 'saints'. We regard them as authentic and as most fully human. Their lives and their individual actions inspire others and encourage us to leave behind a self-centred view of the world and to see ourselves as responsible for the rest of mankind. This is the force of the word 'universal'.

Von Hügel's resolution is also encompassing because he sees it in the context of a whole life. His expression is the word 'mystical', by which he means 'a growth in inner consciousness, a greater awareness of the complexity of feeling and emotion within, which is revealed to us in and through our activity: the people whom we meet, the work we do, what we read and hear and see'. Things

41

are felt from within rather than prescribed (on authority) from outside.

STAGES OF ADULT FAITH

FOWLER	WESTERHOFF	VON HÜGEL
PARADOXICAL–CONSOLIDATIVE UNIVERSALIZING	OWNED	MYSTICAL

J. W. Fowler's long-awaited and most complete study: *Stages of Faith: The Psychology of Human Development and the Quest for Meaning* (Harper and Row, San Francisco, 1981) appeared while we were completing this book. Our most accessible source for a reading of his ideas was J. W. Fowler and Sam Keen: *Life Maps: Conversations on the Journey of Faith* (Word Books, Texas, 1978). John H. Westerhoff's work, *Will our children have faith?* (Seabury Press, New York, 1976) contains the analysis given in this summary.

Some implications of structural development of faith

Von Hügel, Westerhoff and Fowler have all given some systematic description of what can be observed about the nature of faith and its growth. They have each contributed something from their own experience of life which may be of help in meeting the difficulties experienced by parents and teachers with young people. Without our attempting to offer an exhaustive list of implications, the following points are most relevant to our topic of 'growing into faith'. They are itemized because they are all capable of much greater development than space allows here.

1. The dynamic character of faith remains at all stages of life. The searching stage of the adolescent may well 'threaten' the faith of the parents because it questions what has not been previously questioned. It is important to see that this in its turn challenges the faith of parents to grow. The growth is not necessarily perceived as such, but the very pain and difficulty that are experienced may have to be seen 'in faith' as a call from complacency and perhaps unnecessary 'control' over the life of someone called by God to become auto-nomous, to assume personal responsibility.

42

2. While faith needs the security of religion for much of its public liturgical expression, it must also (however paradoxical this sounds!) be able to transcend the limits of religion where these prove to be obstacles to continuing growth. Here there is an immense subject to be considered, but the 'Church always in need of reform' is not one that simply allows for things to happen by official decree. The whole lives of Christians must be prophetic and at times this may have to be at the risk of exposing serious tensions and contradictions within the Church.

3. Faith is always called to grow because the object of faith is God. In our lives we experience differently and as individuals the grace of God and God's continuing revelation of himself through his saving word, the sacraments and the events of our lives. It is especially in our willingness to read God's movement in our individual lives in just these ways, that we see ourselves called to continue to grow more and more deeply into a living faith in him, a faith which shapes and influences our lives, as we listen and respond to the God who speaks and calls.

For personal reflection and group discussion

Some readers may be confused by the technical rather abstract terminology used by the scholars we have quoted to explore the stage-theory notion of growing into faith. It is important to explore these stages as a description of one's own faith journey, that is, to translate the *theory* into *autobiography*. Our Christian heritage offers many examples of such journeys recorded so that they could be shared within the community. Saint Paul offers us such a story within chapter 3 of the Letter to the Philippians, verses 5–16.

Another famous study of 'the road that has brought us forward to where we are' is to be found in the remarkable *Confessions* of Saint Augustine, a book which shows us many ways in which the gift of faith was gradually accepted and came to grow despite the difficulties the author encountered.

Around the year 1100, William of St Thierry, in his book *The Enigma of Faith*, reflected on the passage from Philippians mentioned above, and presented a famous account of faith in the image of a pilgrimage, a comparison already used many times in this book.

Men such as these (the Apostles) walk in faith and even if they are perfect they are travellers; they have not yet reached the end of their journey. They are perfect in that they have forgotten what is behind them and push on to what lies ahead; they are travellers in that they are on a journey. . . .

Once we have embarked upon the path of seeking God, let us not grow weary, let us not stop. He is faithful, who has promised: 'Seek and you shall find.' And the Apostle (2 Cor. 9) says: 'Run so as to obtain the prize.' And he says of himself: 'Brothers, I do not think I have obtained it. But one thing I do, forgetting what is behind and stretching on to what lies ahead, I press on towards the goal, towards the prize of the heavenly calling in Christ Jesus, the Lord.' And he added: 'As many of us who are perfect, let us be of this mind.' What mind? Namely, that as long as we travel far from the Lord, walking by faith, we are travellers and have not reached our destination; and that the perfection of this life consists in being a vigorous traveller in the way of faith. However, the arrival belongs to the next life. Therefore, let us proceed piously and humbly on this path on which we are walking and let us venerate the footsteps of our fathers who have gone before.

(*The Enigma of Faith*, Cistercian Publications, Washington, 1974)

We could go on to cite many other examples but at this stage of our inquiry we think that the *best story* to explore would be your own. And so we invite you to trace the main stages of your personal growth into the faith which is now your own.

4

PERSONAL EXPERIENCE AND GROWTH INTO FAITH

There is not simply one understanding of faith nor only one way of expressing it. The Church is always necessarily engaged in trying to express more deeply, and with all the means at its disposal, the truth about God who sent his Son, Jesus Christ, and left us the assurance of the continuing guidance of the Spirit. Many of us are aware just how our faith has changed during our lives. While there is a sense in which we have 'kept' our childhood faith, we are also aware (as the preceding chapter has set out) that a continuing option for faith has had to be made many times during our lives. Such growth, we have seen, is of the nature of faith itself and distinguishes dynamic *faith* from the more settled and assured things usually associated with *religion*. It is possible, then, that faith and religion which should complement each other can be in tension or even direct opposition. There is such a wide range of possibilities here, as is recognized in Pope Paul VI's words:

> While this first proclamation will be directed primarily towards those who have never heard the good news of Jesus or to children, it will always be needed nevertheless on account of the extent of dechristianization today. Many people who have been baptized live lives entirely divorced from Christianity. It must also be directed to those simple people who have a certain measure of faith but know little even of its fundamental principles. It must extend to intellectuals who feel that they need to approach Jesus Christ from a different standpoint from that which was taught them in their childhood days. . . .
>
> (*Evangelization Today*, pars. 51–2)

This poses the central concern of this chapter. How, in practice, can parents and teachers respect the growing autonomy of young

45

people and at the same time try to provide the conditions which appear to favour growth into a more mature faith? The elements of an answer may be found as we consider the questions raised looking at the importance of a certain continuity between what we will call 'heritage' rather than 'tradition', and the phenomenon of cultural change already looked at in earlier sections.

Different ways of looking at faith

Someone brought up initially in a knowledge and understanding of religion (*the* faith) through a question and answer sequence of a catechism, followed perhaps by a systematic study of an apologetics manual, may well think of his faith as essentially 'doctrine-centred', to use the expression of Jean-Paul Le Berre whose analysis I am following here. Le Berre would describe this attitude as:

> Faith considered as a system that explains the world in totality. At the one time it offers both questions and answers. The questions are posed as unchangeable queries, relevant for all men and for all times, permanently classified.
>
> (*Word in Life*, May 1980, pp. 36–7)

We have seen in an earlier section that this system served the Church so well once in a different kind of society. An historical reflection, however, shows us that such a way of thinking about faith or expressing it, is a long way removed from the attitudes of those Christians whom we encounter in the Acts of the Apostles or the letters of St Paul. They would have expressed faith in another way, much more centred on faith in the person of Jesus Christ and the study of 'all that Jesus said and did'. A third group of modern-day Christians, while not rejecting either of the above approaches, are more inclined to see faith tied to the importance of the unique and historically decisive event of the resurrection of Jesus Christ, and the living history of Christ's continuing presence to the world through his Church. These are three different perspectives which treat the same subject matter, the content of faith. But the modes of expression are very different. Perhaps some of us may recognize ourselves in these different expressions at different times of our lives.

Each of these expressions of faith takes a different approach to the idea of memory. The first, the doctrine-centred, places great importance on the exactness of words which carefully express the understanding of the truths held. So important is this attitude, that there is a tendency to rely on exactly expressed formulae which state the orthodox beliefs to be held by all. This is present also in the second manner of expression, because there is careful attention here to the uniqueness of the Bible and the God who speaks to us through Scripture itself. Both of these approaches rely strongly on the idea of memory as a link with what is past. The third approach also looks to the past, but is more concerned to look at the present too and its continuity in memory with a revelation which continues – for 'God *still* speaks'.

Passing on the heritage

The heritage of the faith, we have just seen, is capable of very diverse cultural expressions. It cannot be reduced to the learning of doctrinal formulae, to specific prayers or to ritual procedures at worship. Pascale's story quoted earlier in this book shows us this only too clearly. But it is obviously urgent that the heirs, the inheritors, must come in some way to experience the richness of their inheritance. 'Do you understand what you are reading?' was Philip's question to the Ethiopian eunuch in the Acts of the Apostles. 'How can I,' was his reply, 'unless some one show me?' How can we show the richness of the heritage as parents and teachers?

The heritage is felt to be alive when it is experienced within living people or within living communities. There can be very many ways of encountering this. For one person, the feeling of transcendence may be generated by viewing a masterpiece of art or a great cathedral; for another, it may be felt in listening to the richness of polyphony or the austere beauty of chant. Various cultural forms are capable of touching the emotions more deeply than words or exhortations, but the sense of awe or of wonder can rest simply at a level of 'culture' too. The ability to open others to new forms of understanding demands rare qualities on the part of parents, teachers and mentors in general, most particularly a certain quality of empathy. As has been indicated already in the discussion of stages of faith, such appreciation cannot be communicated simply by the *authority* of the teacher, at least if this is understood principally in an authoritarian sense. With young people, adults are called to occupy a delicate position of being willing to share personal sensibilities with others, of proposing and sharing, but not of imposing in a categorical way in matters of taste. It is an invitation into a form of sharing of something so obviously treasured and appreciated that it gives a direction to everything in life. Personal responsibility as well as the demands of passing on the heritage are well expressed in the following passage from Pope Paul VI:

> The Church, having been herself sent forth and evangelized, sends out evangelizers in her turn. She teaches them, putting on their lips, as it were, the word of salvation. She communicates to them the message which has been confided to her. She hands on to them the mandate which she has herself received and sends them out to preach, not to preach themselves or their personal ideas, but rather the gospel of which neither they nor the Church herself are the absolute masters, free to dispose of as they wish, but rather the ministers charged to hand it on with complete fidelity. (EN, no. 15)

Let us try to illustrate some important differences between these three different approaches to faith by considering something which can be expressed in different ways in each mode. The example taken will be that of the lives of the saints, such an important illustration of the collective memory of the Church as regards its own history. The monastic tradition required, and still carries out, the reading of a short life of a saint who is honoured by the Church on a particular day. At one level, such an account may read like a fairly mechanical account of someone's life with a basic sequence of dates and events, virtues practised, and reasons for our continuing devotion despite the passage of centuries. A second approach may concentrate on expressing the life of the saint in terms of his response to the gospel, as for example, the lives of St Martin of Tours, the soldier saint who shared his cloak with a poor man on a cold day, or Francis of Assisi who set out to become as close as possible to Christ. These were saints whose lives recall for us their meditation on the words and examples of Christ. In our own day, the example of Mother Teresa of Calcutta seems much more closely related to a third understanding of faith. The faith that brought her to religious life as a young woman, and which led her to make profession within the congregation she had joined, also called her in an insistent way to serve Christ's poor more directly. A notion of faith built around ideas only of 'fidelity' and 'perseverance' was challenged by an insistent call in faith that led her away from her security in a religious congregation to an

48

insecurity of faith. Faith is never only knowledge; it offers a security, but one based on its own nature, that is belief and trust in the God who speaks, calls and saves and not simply on the certainty of knowing.

Mother Teresa may have the capacity to inspire many people today because she seems to embody basic gospel attitudes in today's world. With other possible ways of doing work on behalf of others, she has chosen a way which fills many with admiration. But, charismatic figure that she is, she still uses traditional formulae in her prayers with her sisters, she is obviously steeped in a deep and prayerful knowledge of Scripture, and her life is devoted to making Christ's Kingdom a possibility here on earth for so many of the poor. I think this offers us some important directions in our attempts to help young people grow in faith today. Despite the changes in the society and in the Church, we, of one generation, need to help our young people to claim the rich heritage of which they are the heirs.

Heritage, and not simply tradition

Much of what has been said earlier about cultural change is of great relevance here. Children brought up in Christian families will be introduced to a ritual, a language, a devotional life which often has centuries of tradition behind it. Sometimes, it appears to some young people, there is an appeal to tradition as to some kind of absolute which cannot be examined in any way critically. A good example for many young people would be the traditional music of the Church. Whatever the merits of 'Faith of our Fathers' sung at full volume on St Patrick's Day, it may not have much appeal to many young people who have not known 'the prisons dark' or 'dungeon, fire and sword'. This is still to hope that they may one day come to understand something of the story which is being handed on in such hymns, but also saying that they now need something closer to their own lives. The liturgical changes which brought such transformations as the change from Latin to the vernacular, are now well back in the past of parents and even grandparents. When young people are complaining about liturgy and poor hymns today they are talking about things which have already undergone momentous changes.

Introducing young people into their heritage means many different things, but I think they can be summed up in general by

49

the idea that they must be able to find place for their words and their manner of expression. We should help them to learn to pray, and not be satisfied that this is always accomplished by having them learn prayers. If, as children, they have come to a deep sense of participation in the Eucharist according to the many forms authorized and recommended in the Directory on Masses with Children, we should not conclude that they, only a few years later, will find the standard parish Mass something in which they can become deeply involved. The argument here is not simply for novelty or improvisation. Here are ways in which 'full, active and conscious' participation can be encouraged and continued, but this needs to be seen as a regular necessity and not simply as a concession for certain occasions. The freedom to assume responsibility for some aspects of liturgy, music, readings, processions and so on, is an important form of apprenticeship to learning the deeper meanings of what is to be done (and what is to be avoided) when people are celebrating the Eucharist together.

There is another aspect to all this. Some things in life are only understood from 'inside'. We must remember that many young people simply do not have the vocabulary or the confidence to express to adults what they think or feel about something which touches them greatly. 'It's great', or 'It's not bad', may have to be interpreted sometimes as high praise from some young people. This is not simply a statement about adolescent inarticulateness but also a warning that sometimes they are not quite sure of just what they are *expected* to say!

We think there are particular values of the Christian community which are often communicated to young people when they encounter (to their surprise sometimes!) the spiritual depth in the lives of others. This can happen when young people are associated with some adults in works of helping others, such as traditional sodality work which involves prison visiting or regular, laborious work for the sick or the handicapped. For others, this may occur at the more aesthetic level of participation in some choral work or sharing in music-making which is a sharing also in the value of the kind of work done. What we wish to stress here is that it is the willingness of adults to show a side of themselves which involves feelings and human emotions (and not simply duty) which becomes an important educational – and sometimes deeply spiritual – experience for others.

The 'bridge' of memory

Memory is the bridge between heritage and change. The inheritors of the faith, like their parents and predecessors, have not deserved faith because of any innate merit of their own. They are literally 'graced' by the graciousness of God, but even to begin to see their faith in this way is sometimes a very novel thing for them. We have all heard the adolescent's complaint of 'I never asked to be baptized!', usually uttered when adults are reminding young people of their obligation to do something or not to do something else. In some ways, our whole dialogue with the young is to try to help them see that their 'duty' of being Christian can never be imposed from outside: it is something which is to be welcomed within. And this can never be done until young people have grasped something of their own story and its relationship to the common memory of a family, a church, a people.

When we consider the important use of memory in modern sciences such as psychoanalysis, we begin to see just how subtle and yet how powerful memory can be. Much of the success of certain forms of therapy appears to result from the basic honesty of facing something from the past and not allowing it to exercise a secret and restraining role on present and future actions. This 'healing of memories', as it is often called, is not simply a delving into a past. In the deep sense in which we now refer to the sacrament of penance as the sacrament of reconciliation, we are (as Christ did) reconciling a past and a present to make a freely chosen future, and not one inspired simply by neurosis or guilt.

There is so much of Christian tradition which celebrates this collective memory. It is obviously the central point of the consecration which reminds us that what is being done is 'in memory of me'. Our liturgical feasts tell us of a past in which God entered the lives of the mankind he had freely created. The Bible is full of the accounts of God's great saving plan worked out through the lives of so many people. Perhaps one powerful way of helping the inheritors know their heritage is not simply to read but also to celebrate and pray this saving history. The eleventh chapter of the Epistle to the Hebrews reminds us of the great heroes of the faith whom God supported in their various trials 'through faith'. The restoration of the prayers of intercession into the revised liturgy gives ample scope for small communities to situate themselves and their concerns as a community before God at a moment of worship.

It is impossible to appreciate this sense of being 'heirs' or of there being any heritage unless we, young people and older, make the opportunity to share our own stories – our own family history, our own trials and difficulties in faith, our own need for reconciliation, our own need for support. This is the almost spontaneous origin of what we are now happy to call 'basic communities' and the compelling reason why the Eucharist of small groups and of 'home Masses' has become so important for so many Christians. Recalling memory in *time* also compels us occasionally to limit our *space*: to become a 'little flock', to be able to speak simply to people with whom we are in close proximity. Faith thus speaking to faith, faith speaking to doubt and insecurity and uncertainty, provides the climate where we become more 'owned' by our faith as we continue to grow into it.

The double aspect of being introduced into the heritage (without being locked into tradition) and yet of being open to continuing growth in faith is well summed up by Pope John Paul II in paragraph 60 of *Catechesi Tradendae* in the following words on 'Research and certainty of faith':

> Certain contemporary philosophical schools . . . like to emphasize that the fundamental human attitude is that of seeking the infinite, a seeking that never attains its object. In theology, this view of things will state very categorically that faith is not certainty but questioning, not clarity but a leap in the dark. These currents of thought . . . help us to make the Christian faith not the attitude of one who has already arrived, but a journey forward as with Abraham. However, we must not fall into the opposite extreme, as too often happens. . . . Although we are not in full possession, we do have an assurance and a conviction. . . . It is the search of the Magi under the guidance of a star, the search of which Pascal, taking up a phrase of Saint Augustine, wrote so profoundly: 'You would not be searching for me, if you had not already found me.'

This attitude is one best fostered by an active and encouraging dialogue between different generations. It is demanding upon adults because it can only be carried out when we are prepared to speak openly in faith. This has its risks because convictions learned in the school of experience by adults may not be capable of being perceived, or shared, by younger people. There is a special kind of humility called for in being willing to express one's faith without wishing to impose it on others and at the same time being open to rejection or lack of comprehension. Yet this willingness to share deep and very basic convictions is the only possible basis for a dialogue in faith.

Faith needs encouragement and support

Faith needs the sustaining moments of prayer and retreat, to use two good, old-fashioned Christian words which may need some revaluing. The first, already suggested, must not be equated simply with the saying of set prayers, important though this may be at times also. Nor should we limit the sense of 'retreat' only to a place which is remote and to some kind of prolonged silence. Obviously, there is merit in the peace and quiet of retreat as all religious traditions confirm. With both adults and young people, however, there is much to be said for times when both dialogue and quiet are possible within the same programme. Much of the success of many residential retreat centres for young people in recent years has come about because of the opportunity offered for people to speak together in faith and doubt. This is a profound sharing of oneself most closely associated with Le Berre's third way of expressing faith. God's revelation of himself to me comes through the lives and stories of others who, like me, are made in his image and likeness and have been graced by him throughout their lives. Confidence begets confidence when stories are so shared, because it is only the sense of our mediating the Christ in our midst to one another that encourages us to speak, and to listen, to be filled with wonder and to find new courage. The pattern followed is that of the journey of the disciples to Emmaus, an unexpected journey-meeting with the Lord which leads to a new vision of faith. The implications of this approach were set out in a written intervention to the 1974 Synod of Bishops in Rome by Archbishop John R. Quinn of Oklahoma City:

> When Jesus first met these disciples on the road after his death and resurrection, he asked them what it was that they were so deeply involved in discussing. He listened carefully to their reply as they told him of the events in Jerusalem that had troubled and confused them. When they finished, he responded by beginning to interpret the meaning of the events they had witnessed. Their sharing continued until they reached Emmaus, where the disciples persuaded Jesus to join them for supper. Their encounter culminated in the breaking of the bread in which the disciples recognized their friend as Jesus.

In the same way, youth ministry begins with a *presence* to the young which engenders the confidence and hope to ask questions. *Attentive listening* to the concerns of the young person enables the youth minister to understand more deeply the youth's needs and stage of growth. At that point, the youth minister is able to *respond, sharing* with the young person the help, insights, or values that are the fruit of a life rooted in faith. By *drawing out* of the youth *reflections on the action of God* in the events of his or her own life, this sharing enables the young person to begin formulating answers in the *light of witnessed tradition* and gospel values. The bond created in this relationship is celebrated in community, most fully in the Eucharistic celebration of the Christian community.

If we follow the Emmaus model, youth ministry 'is the Church's mission of reaching into the daily lives of modern young people and showing them the presence of God. . . . It is a return to the way Jesus taught, putting ministry before teaching and people over institutions. In this ministry, religious content is a way of life for the person ministering and the young person touched, through a sequential development of faith, dependent on the readiness and need of the adolescent.'

Those who organize and direct youth programmes recognize that their task is to provide the conditions for a deeper experience of God working in the world in various ways. In listening together to the word of God, in praying privately and with others, in establishing silence so as to hear the voice of God, adults who are prepared to share their faith can free so many young people to express what they feel, and to listen sympathetically to their perceptions about God, about life, about the past and the future. But the contact with others of their own age under circumstances which call for truthfulness and willingness to share still remains one of the most powerful influences of all. Listen to two seventeen-year-olds writing about this:

Sharing my difficulties has left a big impression on me. I've just become aware of something I'd refused to think about previously – my faith is always something being sought after, a continuing questioning, and not something peacefully asleep as I used to think about it.

Every time someone talked about his own faith, I found myself questioning my own faith as well. This questioning has not been easy but I think it has made me more open with myself and with others.

Finally, one obvious challenge of such encounters is the call to discipleship. Once the vision of the Christian life has been seen, there is the invitation to respond. In the language and concepts of the preceding section, it is the challenge to commit oneself resolutely in faith, to allow oneself to be 'owned' by one's faith, and to live, in faith, the consequences of that new certainty.

For personal reflection and group discussion

1. What kind of Church can you envisage which will help *all its members* to continue to grow into faith?
   Is there a gap between the Church you see at present and the kind of Church you think we can try to become?
2. If you were able to do a re-designing exercise on the Church you would like to become:
   – what would you change?
   – why?
3. How does your 'blueprint' compare with that proposed by the young people with whom you are most closely in contact?
4. You may wish to compare your new design for Church with documents produced by the National Pastoral Congress of England and Wales, 1980. See 'The Easter People' and related documents.

5

'NO ONE MAKES THE JOURNEY OF FAITH ALONE'

Our ordinary use of language gives us some insights into some of the different ways we have thought about faith. Sometimes we seem to use it in a way which makes it interchangeable with the word 'religion' as in the following examples:

preserving the faith
defending the faith
holding on to the faith
dying in the faith
losing the faith.

At other times we use it in a way which indicates something more personal:

I place my faith in God.
I have faith in Jesus Christ.
My faith guides me.

As a noun, we can use the same word with very different adjectives:

simple faith, blind faith, good faith, bad faith.

Such expressions help us to appreciate the breadth of faith. Faith includes, yet is more than, *trust*; it is more than a set of beliefs or some norms of conduct; it transcends reason and yet is not unrational. There is something dynamic about faith which always suggests a context of 'doing', rather than something which is passive or static. Faith is a 'doing' word, a living response to the ever-living, active God who never ceases to call us.

It may be a measure of our historical tradition since the Reformation that we have less frequently used expressions such as *celebrating*, *enjoying* or *sharing* our faith. Once again, each expression suggests its own context. Common to all, is the social dimension of a faith held in common by all travellers on the faith journey, as well as the implication that the gift of faith once received cannot remain static. It suggests instead that we are called on frequently to regulate our lives in some way or another in accordance with this gift. This is a fairly obvious point to make, but it is one which the Church seems to have lost sight of at a number of times in history when there was a relative stability and some way of enforcing traditional positions. Within the 'circle' Church, at least so it seems to us now, there was an 'accepted' way of thinking, acting and behaving which was in possession. Anyone trying to act, think or behave in another way was likely to have certain restraints put on him by the general body of opinion within the community. But, to take a recent example, on 11th January 1980 in Catholic Italy, the evening paper, *Corriere della Sera*, invited its readers to consider on the following day the opinions of a number of academics, writers, commentators (including some theologians), to reflect on Pope John Paul II's then recent vindication (or re-vindication) of Galileo in his famous controversy with the Holy Office, and the withdrawing of the right to teach as a Catholic theologian from Professor Hans Küng. The paper is at least hinting at a certain inconsistency here which it now airs for the opinion of certain 'experts', providing at the same time a public forum for its readers to make their own appraisal. I do not wish to do anything more than to use this example as an illustration of the tension between a traditional authority acting within its tradition, and the interpretation put on this action in a pluralist society which no longer accepts forms of censorship or the imposition of restraints on those seeking to explore new ideas. Whatever the 'authorities' may say or do in this matter, the topic is now aired for everyone's *opinion* and this is what will prevail in the long run. It is not fanciful to suggest that this public 'questioning' of the rightness of the Pope's actions would not have taken place in the same way in the Catholic sub-culture of some one or two generations ago. It is this fragmentation within the formerly stable Catholic community which may leave the individual traveller on the journey of faith feeling very much alone.

This is precisely the stage where each person feels the need for the Church, even though the external forms of the Church he knows may not appear to him very helpful. 'No one makes the journey of faith alone', remarked the Italian bishops in their catechetical document of 1970, *Il Rinnovamento della Catechesi*. 'God himself nourishes and strengthens our reflection and our

57

experience of spiritual things, through his Spirit, present in the Church. He sustains each traveller as well with the witness of his brothers and guides him "through the preaching of those who have received, through episcopal succession, the sure gift of truth" ' (Par. 18).

Here is a key concept which needs to be deepened. All of us are travelling on this journey of faith, and we all need the support, encouragement and wise counsel of other travellers who have experienced something more of the route. One central idea of this book is not only that young travellers need the support from an older generation, but equally that older travellers need the vitality, the promise and the hope communicated by the young. In a different society, as we have seen, there were formal structures which ensured a kind of apprenticeship to the great questions of the meaning of life, the importance of God and the role of the Church. In the many-choice society, the need is still apparent, even if we no longer consider that the traditional means are sufficient. What seems certain is that the former model of what we could call in general terms 'socialization' is no longer sufficient, because the passing on of a faith and a value system can only be *begun* by parents with their children, or by teachers with their pupils. The nature of faith itself is such that it must be allowed to grow in freedom, so that an 'experienced' or 'affiliative' faith has to grow past this stage. Faith is more than a quirk of circumstance or of a culture of a particular family.

> Some travel into the mountains accompanied by experienced guides who know the best and least dangerous routes by which they arrive at their destination [says Robert M. Pirsig]. Still others, inexperienced and trusting, attempt to make their own routes. Few of these are successful, but occasionally some, by sheer will and luck and grace, do make it. Once there they become more aware than any of the others that there's no single or fixed number of routes. There are as many routes as there are individual souls.
>
> (*Zen, and the Art of Motor Cycle Maintenance*, Corgi, 1976, p. 181)

Accompanying those who must eventually make their own way. . .

The particular task of parents is to share the early years of the faith journey with their children, that is, to walk with them, to protect them, and to guide them. If the children must eventually find their own paths, they still need experienced guides who can set them on their way. Some aspects of the sharing of experience and the accumulated wisdom of other travellers have already been discussed in the preceding chapter. There is no single method for ensuring that this is successful for we are in the presence of the mystery of each person and the personal relationship with God formed by faith. But there are some constants of accompaniment which need to be repeated.

The first of these is the importance of the celebration of faith which is learned initially through the experience of being part of a faith community. This 'domestic church' of the family, as Pope Paul VI called it, affords the possibility of the experience of a lived faith. Initially, as we have seen, when the child is young, these 'experienced' and 'affiliative' stages are learned largely through imitating others and by coming to prize what is obviously valued within the family. There is an important role of memorizing and repeating basic Christian prayers and actions which nourish the child's faith and offer him security: a place, appropriate ways of acting, and opportunities to participate with other members of the community. What is so learned in the family can be sustained and enlarged in the wider communities of parish and school, although here the sense of the word 'community' needs to be carefully examined. Pope John Paul II writes of this moment of childhood in *Catechesi Tradendae*, pointing out that 'one moment that is often decisive is the one at which the very young child receives the first elements of catechesis (instruction) from its parents and the family surroundings. These elements will perhaps be no more than a simple revelation of a good and provident Father in heaven to whom the child learns to turn its heart' (Par. 36). And yet, if the child has not had the experience of such a living faith shared and 'learned' in some way in the family, school can be difficult and indeed harsh because of the child's unfamiliarity with what is considered normal. A teacher, born in Italy but brought to Australia as a young child, recalls:

My experiences in the second grade at the local Catholic school were unhappy. I can recall my first communion day simply because one nun admired my frock and because we had jelly at the communion breakfast. I was slapped many times for not knowing my prayers as the others did and for not being able to tell my teacher how many persons there were in the Blessed Trinity.

A second constant in accompanying those who must eventually assume personal responsibility is a deep respect for their personal freedom at all times. This seems so basic that it is heavily underlined in many official statements since the Second Vatican Council, most notably in the Decree on Religious Freedom in the following excerpts.

The search for truth, however, must be carried out in a manner that is appropriate to the dignity of the human person and his social nature, namely, by free inquiry with the help of teaching or instruction, communication and dialogue. . . .

Moreover it is by personal assent that men must adhere to the truth they have discovered. . . (Par. 2 Flannery).

One of the key truths in Catholic teaching, a truth that is contained in the word of God and constantly preached by the Fathers, is that man's response to God by faith ought to be free, and that therefore nobody is to be forced to embrace the faith against his will. . . . It is fully in accordance with the nature of faith that in religious matters every form of coercion by men should be excluded (Par. 10).

The particular task required of parents (and teachers) is to balance up this basic respect for the freedom of children with their parental responsibility to ensure that the faith is known. Pope Paul VI pointed up the dilemma and its possible resolution in his letter 'Evangelization Today':

It is certainly wrong to force anything on the conscience of our brothers. But it is quite another matter to present to their consciences the gospel truth and salvation in Jesus Christ clearly, while fully respecting their freedom of choice and election – 'excluding every form of action which appears to savour of coercion or dishonest or undue persuasion' (Par. 4)

So far from this being a violation of liberty or conscience it is a mark of respect for that liberty when we give the opportunity of choosing a way of life which seems noble and praiseworthy even to those who do not believe in God. . . (Par. 80).

Celebrating faith needs a community

A third constant of accompaniment is the need for a community. It has already been suggested that many people who seem to reject the Church appear to be seeking what the Church exists to offer. This is particularly true of the basic need for acceptance and welcome within a community. Just as the child's first experiences of faith ideally take place in the natural community of the family, so too they are often continued in the experience of parish and of school. In both instances, however, the determining factor seems to be whether or not they experience both of these institutions, to some extent at least, as communities. Where the school is avowedly Christian, the child continues to be introduced to the experience of prayers and hymns in common, and to the various manifestations of faith by the adults responsible for the school or a particular group. In the spirit of the Directory on Mass with Children, such celebrations of liturgy invite a whole-hearted participation by all members of the congregation. Attention to careful planning around a central theme can often result in much more active participation than is usually the case with adults.

It is much the same with the preparation and celebration of liturgy throughout primary schools, so much so that it has often been remarked that young people who do not normally attend Sunday liturgies in a parish, often enjoy participating with others in a school celebration. This sense of being part of a community and of the community's celebration of the faith which unites it together is so important that we need to reflect on some of its characteristics. Where people are known by their names, where they participate by their presence, their voices, their postures and gestures, in a celebration where they understand (because of preparation of the readings and their participation in a dialogue homily with their teacher or celebrant), the transcendent dimension of being part of the sacrifice of the Mass is much more likely to be felt and appreciated. This does not mean necessarily that those participating are any more coherent in explaining what they have done. The proof is rather in their presence and in their willingness to continue to be present for such celebrations.

A similar point could be made about the experience of a residential retreat or weekend with young people. Experienced workers in such centres point to the central importance of the liturgy celebrated. It seems ironical, therefore, to encounter some forms of opposition to such programmes centred around shared experience on the grounds that they do not help young people to

61

return to the kind of liturgy they will encounter in their own parish. It seems that for many young people the important 'experience' of a pastoral centre or week-end retreat is the beginning of some understanding of what 'church' might be! The opportunities for prayerful reflection and group discussion all prepare the way for the celebration of faith – and of doubt, of uncertainty – in liturgy. There is the problem of having to return to the reality of a more formal, more structured and often duller church than the one they have just experienced. It could be hoped that the very 'high' experienced by young people could be the basis for a sharing and development of more 'active and conscious' liturgical participation in the parish, rather than being regarded as something dangerously 'unsettling' for them.

When liturgy and the celebration of faith lose the sense of a present tense (*this* celebration, *this* moment, *this* emphasis, *these* people) they are easily reduced to the level of ritual, at least in the minds and attitudes of many young people who, like Pascale, attend for vague reasons which are good in themselves, only to find themselves unwelcome, isolated spectators at something in which they feel themselves strangers.

This point is clearly recognized in the U.S. Bishops' *Vision of Youth Ministry*:

> Youth ministry must be a living interaction between God and young people, an event that *remembers* the personal and religious events of the past and *initiates* even deeper involvement for future becoming, but always celebrates the present relationships as the young person praises, sings, shouts, or whispers 'Amen'.
>
> (Section E. Components of Youth Ministry, 1976)

Faith or religion?

A fourth constant of accompaniment for those on the faith journey is to recognize that younger as well as older travellers may become distanced from formal religion in their quest for faith. This seems paradoxical, and perhaps highly dangerous, but, as has been suggested at a number of points in this book, the static elements in religion can appear to be opposed to the dynamic growth of faith.

The following extract from an article by John Harriott, called 'Lapsing From School', illustrates a common sequence:

The route to lapsing follows an all-too-familiar pattern. Commandments are assimilated as absolute rules: to break these rules is to be separated from God's love for ever, death of the soul. As the child reaches puberty he finds himself, or believes himself to be, breaking one of these rules, usually those to do with sex or missing Mass. He may go to confession, though often enough he does not because he is too ashamed or too inarticulate to express himself, but even if he does he finds that his temptations are not dissipated overnight. He continues to go to Mass but fears that communion would be sacrilegious. A sense of alienation from the community sets in, and with it a sense of isolation and hopelessness. Mass becomes a painful routine and is finally abandoned. Another young Catholic has given up the practice of his faith without, perhaps, quite losing it.

(The Month, December 1968, p. 311)

In arguing for an approach by parents and teachers which recognizes that

it is not merely knowing a commandment as one might know, say, the l.b.w. law (in cricket), but recognizing it as a law of life to do with being a totally alive human being, which is the heart of the matter, for it is not the notional assent of the mind, but the assent of the heart which makes a moral man. (ibid. p. 312),

the same author shows two aspects of the problem:

Fear of laxity, of taking away some jot or tittle of the Law, at least proceeds from a conscientious motive which deserves respect: less admirable is an intolerance and impatience which stem from a desire for visible, if only apparent, success (which can lead to lifting every temptation from a child's path, dragooning in virtue, and an iron discipline which makes breaches of school as well as moral rules impossible), and, worse, a complete failure to understand the essence of Christian virtue and how the need for a minimum of public order within a community can divert attention from our whole purpose which is to teach people how to love (ibid. p. 313).

Just as it is important not to allow the ethical or moral dimension of religion to become predominant, so too for its other dimensions. For example, it is possible for young people to associate the idea of *doctrine* with abstract formulations about God which effectively hide for them the living sense of the God who has revealed himself. People can learn a language *about* God but never have the sense of encountering God in a personal relationship. These are all real dangers posed by the formal, institutional, organized aspects of religion: they are the difficulties experienced not only by young people, but there are particular reasons why the young remain suspicious of anything which is not supported by the example of those recommending it.

Pope Paul VI was uncompromising in making this same point:

Let us now consider the preachers of the gospel themselves. It is often said that our age is thirsting for sincerity and honesty. Young people in particular are said to have a horror of falsity and hypocrisy and to seek above all truth and clarity.

These 'signs of the times' should convince us of the necessity for the utmost vigilance. We are constantly being questioned, sometimes tacitly, sometimes openly: Do you believe yourselves what you are saying to us?

Is your life in accord with your beliefs?

Is your preaching in accord with your life?

(*Evangelization Today*, Par. 76)

There is an important point to be made here, however, about the sustaining aspects of religion. The common experience of so many people seems to be the way in which they are challenged at different moments of their lives by the searching questions posed by life itself with its unresolved dilemmas, by the mysteries of pain, suffering, and death. Being 'owned' or 'possessed' by faith will often require a personal ratification of that ownership in times of suffering and great personal darkness. This is not a time when there are answers to be found. Frequently, it seems, support is found in the sustaining presence of others, in the repetition of well-tried prayer formulae, in clinging to a faith which appears to demand too much from us.

This is a particular form of accompaniment which the more experienced travellers should try to share with their younger associates. We are not the first or the only people on earth. Perhaps all we can do at times is to try to accept the questioning of the young, not in terms of providing answers, but in sharing the anguish which gives rise to the questions. This quiet wisdom is that of experience. It is offered not in terms of an answer, but in empathy with the questioner. It is offered not from the dominating position of one who has found an answer, but from the truthful humility of one who has not. Being able to rely on the prayer of the whole Church, being able to trust the experience of those who have gone before us, is where religion can sustain us and complements the searching dynamic of faith.

Can we try to express this in terms of our journeying images as follows? Because the journey of faith is long, the wisdom of those who have preceded us has seen the necessity for the inn or the oasis to break the journey. The place and the company afford us travellers' tales, rest, food and drink. The constant temptation is to want to end the journey, and to mistake the resting place for the journey's end. But the inn and the oasis are still important places which teach us many things and refresh us for the uncompleted journey still to come.

A postscript

To grow into faith is to hear God's call; it is to become a disciple of Jesus, to make what Paul VI (in his fine Holy Year letter, 'Christian Joy', 1975) describes as a 'journey to the inner place where the Father, the Son and the Holy Spirit welcome one into their own intimacy and divine unity. "If anyone loves me, my Father will love him, and we shall come to him and make our home with him." To reach this presence always presupposes a deepening of true knowledge of oneself as a creature and as a child of God. Was it not an inner renewal of this kind that the recent Council fundamentally desired? We have here a work of the Spirit, a gift of Pentecost.'

The work of the Spirit is also the work of the church-communities: to open ways into the 'inner place' and to offer maps for the journey. In *Gaudium et Spes*, the Vatican Council asserted that the mission of the Church is 'to reveal the mystery of God, who is the ultimate goal of man' (*Gaudium et Spes* 41); the Pastoral Constitution continues:

> In doing so it opens up to him the meaning of his own existence, the innermost truth about himself. . . . The Church realizes that man is continually being aroused by the Spirit of God and that he will never be utterly indifferent to religion – a fact confirmed by the experience of past ages and by plentiful evidence at the present day. For man will ever be anxious to know, if only in a vague way, what is the meaning of his life, his activity, and his death. The very presence of the Church recalls these problems to his mind. The most perfect answer to these questionings

is to be found in God alone, who created man in his own image and redeemed him from sin; and this answer is given in the revelation of Christ his Son who became man. Whoever follows Christ the perfect man becomes himself more a man.

To grow into faith is to become more human – by following Christ the perfect man. Our Church is entrusted with this message as good news for all mankind. To grow into faith is to grow to realize that the good news is given to me not just for myself but to share it with others, believers and non-believers. Since the Vatican Council, Christians have grown to see this more clearly. The 1975 Letter on *Evangelization*, quoted many times in this book, asserts emphatically that we are all called to pass on to others the saving word and call spoken to us and through us. In Scripture, God's word is often described in other striking metaphors: it is *light*, *power*, *life*, *love*. . . .

If I think of the word as *light*, then I will think of evangelization as *illumination* (so I can *see* differently); if I see the word as *power*, as Paul often does, then I will perhaps think of evangelization as *liberation* (as many Latin American churches do) and I will realize the challenge this brings to the way I relate to the human struggle for freedom and justice. Pope Paul asserted strongly that 'the Church's work of evangelization must deal with community life in society, with the life of all nations, with peace, justice and progress. It must deliver a message about liberation . . . proclaiming the liberation of hundreds of millions of people, helping this liberation, bearing witness on its behalf, assuring its full development' (EN 29, 30).

If I think of the word as *life*, then I may see evangelization as a process of *healing* or even *awakening* from a dead or half-dead state, a call to live more fully, to break through the paralysing effects of depression or failure. If I hear the word as *love*, as a word of *acceptance*, God's acceptance of me as I am, then his *yes* to me will be the good news that I belong, that I am not an outcast, that 'I'm OK'. This may be the good news that everyone needs to hear many times in life, but especially in adolescence, where many of the cries of youth are howls of pain and rejection. To hear God's word as good news, as positive affirmation, will set me free to say *yes* to myself and *yes* to others, and thus to say *yes* to the future.

I can discover this only from experience, never from textbooks or formulae. We could define evangelization as *God's word spoken and heard in a given culture*. In the early parts of this book, we explored the given culture that is ours – a culture that needs to be questioned, explored, and challenged by the word of God. I may think of myself as one who *speaks* God's word to the young whose task is to *listen*, to *hear* the message that I speak. This view is partial and inadequate. My task is also to be a listening person, called to help the young to become articulate, called to liberate the word in them. Through their questions and their yearnings, complaints and hopes, God may be speaking to me, calling me to grow into a faith which is more sensitive, more aware and more Christlike.

So what about this vision of a living Church, which is good news for a world so often disillusioned by the failures and inadequacies of religious systems which seem to preach one thing while prac- tising another? How does it compare with the sad old lady, dress- ing up for the hollow celebrations, while the young yawn with boredom? It's a long way off. . . . And yet, in the last few years, there have been so many promising signs of a renewal of faith and of community in the most unlikely places, sometimes in the very centre of decay and hopelessness. Our age has its prophets, like every other. God still speaks, and his word has lost none of its power. It is a word many young people long to hear:

> I want the Church to show me the love and glory of God himself, so that, with God's help, the Church, society, and the world will work itself out – through God's love,
>
> > wrote one seventeen-year-old recently.

And one of the great Christian poets of our age, R. S. Thomas, already quoted in this book, takes up the cry of, 'It's a long way off!', and opens up a glimpse of something which may be closer to us than we think . . . if . . . IF. . . .

THE KINGDOM

> It's a long way off but inside it
> There are quite different things going on:
> Festivals at which the poor man
> Is king and the consumptive is
> Healed; mirrors in which the blind look
> At themselves and love looks at them
> Back; and industry is for mending
> The bent bones and the minds fractured
> By life. It's a long way off, but to get
> There takes no time and admission
> Is free, if you will purge yourself

Of desire, and present yourself with
Your need only and the simple offering
Of your faith, green as a leaf.

(from *H'm*, Macmillan 1972)

The 'if' is always there – the necessary condition: an honest admission of need, a readiness to grow, shown in the *simple offering* of a personal faith, which, like a tree, grows through seasons of change, but keeps emerging into a new springtime of fresh, green life. This is a faith to be shared with others at very special festivals. These are happening everywhere. Have you noticed?

Paul's prayer for the Christian community at Ephesus takes up the image which we have made the central image of this book: the image of *growth*. His prayer opens up an awe-inspiring vision of what happens to individuals and communities as they grow into faith. It is with this vision that we end our exploration of the questions facing one generation of Christians as we try to grow into the future.

This is what I pray,
kneeling before the Father,
from whom every family, whether spiritual or natural takes its name:
Out of his infinite glory,
may he give you the power through his Spirit
for your hidden self to grow strong,
so that Christ may live in your hearts through faith,
and then, planted in love and built on love,
you will with all the saints have strength
to grasp the breadth and the length,
the height and the depth;
until, knowing the love of Christ which is beyond all knowledge,
you are filled with the utter fullness of God.

Glory be to him
whose power, working in us,
can do infinitely more than we can ask or imagine;
glory be to him
from generation to generation
in the Church and in Christ Jesus
for ever and ever. Amen.

(Ephesians 3: 14–21)

For personal reflection and group discussion

1. As you come to the end of this book, can you choose some New Testament references which illustrate a basic idea of this book, namely, that our faith is our way of responding always to our God
   – who speaks
   – who calls
   – who saves?
   Are there any gospel incidents in which you see yourself reflected?
2. If you try to represent your own faith journey to the present moment by some kind of diagram, or a sequence of quotations from the Bible,
   – what does your diagram look like?
   – how does it help you to understand your relationship in faith to young people?
3. The Church, too, is on a journey of faith . . . 'the way' (Acts 9:2). Where does 'the way' appear to be leading you now? Are you willing to follow? What of the young people you know? Are you willing to invite others to share your journey?